Can I Quote You on That?

The Interview Process from Start to Finish

BearManor Media.com

Typesetting and layout by PKJ Passion Global

Published in the USA by
BearManor Media
P1317 Edgewater Dr #110
Orlando FL 32804
www.BearManorMedia.com

Softcover Edition
ISBN-10:
ISBN-13: 979-8-88771-262-8

Published in the USA by Bear Manor Media

This book is dedicated to my mother.
Thank you so much for all the conversations.

Contents

Acknowledgements

Cover image "Skunkie" generously provided by Marilyn Nesbitt

Cover image scan courtesy of The Framemakers' Gallery in Leesburg, Florida

Preface

Although most of the people I have interviewed are actors, directors, and people who make movies, my first two interviews were with musicians. On a warm summer night on June 8, 1996, I interviewed lead singer and guitarist Kevin ("Kevn") Kinney of Driving N Cryin. My undergraduate college in Thomasville, Georgia had an annual outdoor music festival called Day on the Green that drew thousands of people. I wrote short articles and music reviews for *The Talon*, Thomas University's—then Thomas College's—newspaper, and I posed the idea of interviewing the band. I thought it would be good for the newspaper and a way for me to meet the group whose music I knew something of from MTV and the radio. After they played, Kinney sat outside on the ground with me and a few other people. Everyone seemed scared to talk to him. Nobody said anything; we just sat there looking at him. He casually started talking about his life, the band, and music. I asked him a couple of questions along the way. I can't remember if I had any questions prepared or not. I know I didn't have a tape recorder. I may have jotted down a few quotes from him—or maybe I went from memory or even an approximation thereof—as there are some sprinkled in the published piece, which ended up as more of an article than an interview. The whole experience was probably closer to an extended meet and greet than a conventional interview. "Laidback" would be a diplomatic way to describe my approach. However, "well-intentioned but virtually unprepared" is a more accurate summation. Well, it was a start, and I did have a cool experience. I felt pretty good about the whole thing, all factors considered.

About a year later, on a pleasant late spring evening on May 31, 1997, I interviewed Creed for their Day on the Green appearance. This go-around I think I had some questions prepared, but that was it. We sat inside and talked before the show. The whole band was present, but lead singer Scott Stapp did most of the talking. Shortly into the interview, an employee of the college loaned me a micro-cassette recorder. This was especially fortunate because we were sitting at a round table with individual shot glasses and a bottle of Jägermeister standing in a bowl of ice in the center of the table; the drinks enhanced my mood but probably not my memory. At the end of the interview, I recall the entire band signing a glossy promo photo they gave me—I still have that—and then patiently waiting while I related a personal story of my own that I felt was relevant to them and their music. I imagine it's the sort of experience they had all the time with fans. Though they didn't say much after, they did seem to listen intently to what was probably a variation of something they had already heard many times, and I will always appreciate their patience. This interview felt semi-professional, and I think I did a little better with Creed than with Kinney. At least I had more material.

The first quarter of the article—I saved it, too—that I wrote gives a little of Creed's history and describes the show. The rest of it consists of two questions I asked about spiritual/religious influence on their music and whether the experience of success is what they thought it would be like (not incredibly unique questions, but on-point at least). Rather than transcribing the entire conversation and then editing, I remember focusing on typing those two questions and answers for the article. I can't remember why; maybe they seemed the most polished. I don't think I really did much editing. There aren't any speech fillers and there is little repetition in the final version, but I think I pretty much transcribed what Stapp said and put his words in the piece as they came out of his mouth, so any strength in my article is probably due much less to my editing abilities at that time and more to his conversational skills. Good thing he was well-spoken.

Twila Maxwell-Gibson, then a fellow student of mine and friend, suggested using the rest of the tape for an interview and giving it to a magazine in Tallahassee, where Creed were from. It was a great idea that I wish now I had pursued, but I had no idea how to proceed or how to even get in touch with any publications (the internet existed, but only one computer at the College had it, and I wouldn't get on the internet for the first time until later that year in another town). It didn't occur to me until a few minutes ago when I was locating that old signed promo photo from Creed that there is contact information for management and promoters that includes two phone numbers and two email addresses (I wonder if they still work?). Those folks might have helped me with placing the rest or part of the rest of the interview. While I didn't have internet or a phone (yes, landlines existed, but I didn't have one, let alone a cell-phone), it probably didn't matter. I was too scared to try. I didn't want to push my luck, as if I was worried someone was going to come around and revoke my first interview, expose me as a fraud, and punish me for trying. Anxiety, I suppose, and lack of confidence.

Somewhere over the years the tape disappeared; it's possible I knowingly threw it out thinking I would never have any further use for it, and I didn't have the equipment to play it anyway. While I doubt the complete interview could ever have, say, become the cover story for an issue of *Rolling Stone*, I could have done something more with it—even now—and if nothing else, I'd love to hear my college-self talking with and hanging out with a 1990s rock band.

Later that year, Creed would make a fall in-store appearance at Tracks, a music store at the small local strip mall near the edge of town. Bands from out of town did not come to Thomasville very often. I remember a girl on her cellphone saying, "There's a million people here!" and someone else saying, "Thomasville translation: fifty." Obviously nervous without the electric instruments, amplification, onsite personnel, instrument techs, a sound or line check, monitors, and all the usual things they were used to having for live performances, Creed played a couple of acoustic songs in the parking lot to a crowd that had dwindled to about a dozen of us for the live set. People were enthusiastic. I still remember people cheering when Creed started playing "My Own Prison," which was their big song at the time. I wish I had tried to interview them as they were packing away their equipment, away from the crowd, the loud amplifiers, and the booze of the summer before.

A year later they would release their debut album. *My Own Prison* went on to sell six million copies. Their next album sold nearly double that. Depending on your source, Creed has sold forty million to fifty-three million total albums worldwide. Despite the massive record sales, chart-topping hits, videos on heavy rotation, and world tours, I'll always remember that vulnerable, self-conscious band in a small-town parking lot, Scott Stapp barely making eye contact, and then pulling away immediately if anyone caught his eye. That moment will never come again. And I was there for it.

Introduction

In a sense, we are always interviewing people. Even when we are thinking to ourselves, we are often interviewing ourselves, asking ourselves questions, trying to get to the bottom of something, determining how we feel about some circumstance or person, striving for clarity, framing a narrative, thinking over the intricacies of a point, making connections, working on or working out a problem in our own mental spaces, processing the past, struggling with the present, and thinking through options about the future.

Our daily conversations may be brief, impromptu, and not always particularly deep, but they are still interviews, and there is some purpose to the conversation. We are trying to get an internal view of some sort, a look or even just a glimpse inside of another person whether it is their view of the nature of the cosmos, how the Fightin' Armadillos of Iceland are doing at curling this year, or just how their general day is going.

Interviews—like people—seem pretty simple on the surface. You get some questions together, you ask those questions, and you write out what the other person says. A lot of things seem simple on the surface. You have students, you teach them. You have children, you raise them. You have plants, you plant and water them. You have a pet, you feed and clean up after the pet. You have a life, and you live it. However, as anyone who has attempted any of these things knows, it's a lot more complicated than that. There is a whole lot of other work you have to do that nobody tells you about and every situation is unique. Interviews are no different.

If you just make a list of questions, go through your questions, and transcribe what the other person says, yes, you'll have an interview, but unless you are very lucky, you probably won't have a very good one, or at least it won't be as good as it could be if you apply certain techniques that we'll talk about. Conducting the actual interview can be the easiest part of the process. The real labor often comes before and after the interview.

A Note About Identities, Terms, Structure, and Liability

There may be times I sound deliberately vague about people's identities. This may be because either I do not want to sound negative or I don't want to say something potentially embarrassing about them or share an experience with them that they did not intend to become general knowledge. I continue to appreciate and thank anyone who has ever given me or helped me get an interview; nobody owed it to me or anyone else. In a few situations, I don't want to reveal exactly who connected me with someone who might be especially popular because I do not want that person to become besieged with requests to connect them, too (NEVER connect someone to an interviewer without the potential interviewee's permission). Also, I am going to talk around the edges of a few ideas I never pursued and did not complete but might in the future, so I want to hold those back for myself.

I'll explain terms along the way. The main one you need to know is *interviewee*. The interviewee is the person the interviewer interviews. You may run across the term *subject* in other places. Originally, I used that so that I could switch terms in and out. Besides the risk of confusion between *subject* as an interviewee and *subject* as the topic of something, something about *subject* sounds cold, inhuman, and clinical to me.

I've structured this book just like the title implies: chronologically. However, you can flip around as you like. Maybe you already know whom you want to talk to, so you can skip to that section. Perhaps you have finished interviews and are in the editing process, so the sections about and examples of editing matter more to you. Go ahead and jump over to that. I considered creating an index, but I think an index would be redundant because I've given clear section headings, so use those and the table of contents to guide you.

You use any of the ideas in here and apply any of the content in these pages completely at your own risk. Nothing in here is a guarantee or intended as legal advice. If you have any legal questions or concerns, consult an attorney.

Get Organized

When I was a kid, I just kind of remembered everything. As a teacher, I tend to make handwritten notes on my syllabi and go by those. Sometimes I send an email to myself as a reminder or text myself short phrases. As an adult, I have little use for a daily planner; most days my life isn't organized in fifteen minutes blocks. I tried a planner, but the main issue I have is that a planner doesn't give me a single, comprehensive view of my present and future plans. I keep a running document in Word that has a list of appointments, trips, reminders, and ongoing projects. It tends to run about two to three pages at any given time, and it doesn't contain any columns, charts, graphics, or color coordination. "1_a to do list" (minus the quotation marks) is the name of the document. The "1_a" keeps it at the top of Word, and I always have it as a pinned document also. Any big project—anything more than about fifteen pages—gets its own folder and Excel spreadsheet. If you are working on a single interview, you probably don't need a separate folder and spreadsheet.

If you are working on multiple interviews, then you probably do. The best and easiest time to develop a method of organization is at the very start of a project; that's why I put this section first. It becomes very easy very quickly to forget you just bugged that person last night or you have forgotten about them and it's been six months. Did you ever get the consent form back or not? Did you even send it? Somebody said they had photos from the set, but who was that, and did you ever receive them? At best, you will waste time going back through emails or your call log trying to recreate the individual timeline for a specific interviewee. At worst, you will either seem pushy when you pester someone about something you just asked them about two days ago or the opposite will happen and something will fall through the cracks and remain forgotten.

Organizational and measurement systems can also be splendid timewasters and methods of procrastination. You can spend/waste endless amounts of time learning about, tinkering with, and creating categories and formulas. Remember that a spreadsheet is a means to an end, not an end in itself. The purpose of the spreadsheet is to keep the most important information in a central, easy-to-find and easy-to-read location and save you time. It is a tool to help you with the major project; it is not the major project itself. The only way to actually get work done is to get work done.

The spreadsheet doesn't need much. Mine is very basic. At the tops of the columns, I use the following headings: Interviewee, Interviewee Copy, Signed Consent, Notes, Contact Information, and Pages. Interviewee (Column A) refers to the name of the interviewee. I also include the date I conducted the interview. Interviewee Copy (Column B) refers to the status of the interview and provides a space to record relevant information. Have I sent a copy to the interviewee? When did I send it? Did I get it back, but I need to do something else to it? Is it finished? If I need to forward it to someone else, did I do that yet? If so, when did I do it? Signed Consent (Column C) refers to the status of the consent/release form. Did I send it? When did I send it? Did I get it back yet? If I need to forward it to someone else, did I do that yet? If so, when did I do it? I usually devote the equivalent of two columns to record Notes (Columns D and E). The Notes column consists of any relevant information not in any of the other columns. For example, did someone say they have photographs or other images? What's the status of those? Did someone mention another person I should talk to or source to look at? Is the interviewee leaving for a five-week trip to Europe two weeks from now? Contact Information (Column F) should list phone numbers and email addresses. I always like having a sense of my own progress, so the final column I include is Pages (Column G), which refers to the number of pages of the finished interview. I use the top of the next column for the Total Pages (Column H) and include a simple Excel formula =SUM(G2:G150), for example, to total the pages. This is also useful so that I know how many total pages I have when I am still keeping each interview in its own file. Knowing how many pages I have completed gives me a nice and motivating sense of progress, too. I space the columns so that I can see all categories without scrolling to the left or right, so I just have to scroll up and down to see the top and bottom of the page, depending on how many interviewees I have. I insert and keep at least one blank row between each person's block of information. Make it easy to read. Give it room to breathe.

This is pretty quick and easy to set up, will keep you organized, and will save loads of time if you are working on a larger project or multiple smaller projects. After a couple of interviews, you will appreciate being able to open a single file and see the basic information laid out and easy-to-find right in front of you. Just remember to periodically email it to yourself or keep another copy backed up somewhere—as you should with all documents related to the interview or interviews. Like anything else, this is just a model, one possible version. Modify or tweak so that it best serves you.

Make and Maintain a Portfolio

It's beneficial to gather and update a collection of your interviews. You may want to review and enjoy your accomplishments. A more practical reason is that you may be asked for proof of your experience and credentials in consideration for an interview. There is not a single correct way to format the information but once you decide on a way, stick with it and be internally consistent. Include basic information (title of the collection or publication, name of the interviewee, and date) along with a link to the book or article, if available. If it's in a book, link to it on Amazon or wherever the public can purchase it. People should at least be able to find your name on the cover or somewhere in the front matter via the preview function if they cannot read the entire book online. If the interview appears online as part of a magazine or other publication, you should always take screenshots of your online work (I use the Print function and when the Print screen comes up, I select the "Microsoft Print to PDF" option in Printer). Arrange your list chronologically starting with the most recent interview. I place any links on a new line, just under the interview. I like to include bullet points. I attach screenshots to the email and set them up so that their order matches their placement in my list. I attach the list to the email and place it in the body of the email. Make it easy for the reader. What follows is not a complete list of my interviews, but a partial list that will show you how I document and format my credentials to share with someone else. Make it clean, clear, concise, organized, and easy-to-read:

SINGLE INTERVIEWS

- Interview with Keith Hamilton Cobb Part I. *Aji Magazine* 16 Spring (2022).
  www.ajimagazine.com/uploads/2/2/2/8/22289112/2022-v3-aji_magazine_spring_2022_issue_16.pdf
- Interview with David Kirby. *Aji Magazine* 15 Fall (2021).
  www.ajimagazine.com/uploads/2/2/2/8/22289112/ajimaga-zinefall2021issue15-final.pdf

- Interview with Craig Blackwell. *The Rockpit* (3/15/2021). https://www.therockpit.net/2021/interview-craig-blackwell-guitarist-todd-la-torre/
- Interview with Todd La Torre. *The Rockpit* (2/25/2021). https://www.therockpit.net/2021/interview-todd-la-torre-queensryche-solo-artist/
- Interview with Robert Englund *Fantha Tracks* (1/21/2020). Reprinted in *The Media HQ*. https://www.fanthatracks.com/interviews/interview-robert-englund-and-his-star-wars-connection/
- Interview with Leigh Rourks. *Aji Magazine* 10 Spring (2019). www.ajimagazine.com/issue-10-spring-2019.html click "(online) free" and a PDF of the issue will open.
- Interview with The Crystal Method. *PopMatters* (9/12/2018). https://www.popmatters.com/crystal-method-2018-interview-2604136815.html
- Interview with Sin Quirin of Ministry. *Brutal Resonance* (3/25/2018). https://www.brutalresonance.com/interview/sin-quirin-mar-2018/

INTERVIEW COLLECTIONS

- *Roger Corman's New World Pictures (1970-1983): An Oral History. Volume 2.* Associate Editor. BearManor Media, 2020. Interviews with Martin Kove, Robert Englund, Alex Hajdu, and Barry Schrader. https://www.amazon.com/gp/product/1629336068/ref=dbs_a_def_rwt_hsch_vapi_thcv_p1_i1
- *Roger Corman's New World Pictures (1970-1983): An Oral History. Volume 1.* Associate Editor. BearManor Media, 2020. Interviews with Grace Zabriskie, Sid Haig, and Durinda Wood. https://www.amazon.com/gp/product/1629335770/ref=dbs_a_def_rwt_hsch_vapi_thcv_p1_i0

- *Forsaken: The Making and Aftermath of Roger Corman's The Fantastic Four*. General Editor. BearManor Media, 2019. Rendered as an audiobook on 6/23/2022 by Punch Audio with much of the original cast reading. https://www.amazon.com/Forsaken-Aftermath-Cormans-Fantastic-hardback/dp/1629335045/ref=sr_1_4?dchild=1& keywords=forsaken+fantastic&qid=1619454968&sr=8-4

Though one can argue that we might be considering details a bit too finely, I think the preceding format, in which all the information lines up under the first line, looks and reads a little better than the next format in which all the information lines up with the left margin and is indented like a paragraph:

- *Forsaken: The Making and Aftermath of Roger Corman's The Fantastic Four*. General Editor. BearManor Media, 2019. Rendered as an audiobook on 6/23/2022 by Punch Audio with much of the original cast reading. https://www.amazon.com/Forsaken-Aftermath-Cormans-Fantastic-hardback/dp/1629335045/ref=sr_1_4?dchild=1& keywords=forsaken+fantastic&qid=1619454968&sr=8-4

If you are not already collecting your work, go ahead and start; it will not be any easier later on and you want to be sure to capture any online interviews while you can in case the publication ceases operation and the site disappears. Once you collect all of it, just add future interviews and publications as they come in. Maintaining the list is easier than scrambling to try to remember, collect, and organize what you have done when suddenly called upon to present your credentials.

Whom Do You Talk To?

If you have been assigned an interview with a specific person, then the answer is obvious. However, if you are working on a project about a film or a television series, then the short answer is: Talk to everyone you can. The initial impulse is to seek out the "top" people such as the director and the main actors. Obviously, they are deeply connected to the film, they are the first names that come to the minds of a general audience and readership, and there is something of a prestige factor associated with the names of people who appear on movie posters. However, there are other groups of people with great stories to tell: for example, people who worked on the soundtrack, actors with less screen time, special effects people, wardrobe designers, and scriptwriters. Different roles bring different perspectives. These folks can be easier to find contact information for, may not have been interviewed quite so much, and have unique behind-the-scenes information. In short, people with less visible or small roles may have big stories.

IMDB (Internet Movie Database) is a good first place to look for films. Once you type in the name of a movie, you will see a page that lists the director, writer(s), and some of the cast members. Then, you can click on links to show every name that worked on the film and every role/position. The list will often include uncredited roles, so in that way it's more exhaustive than the actual credits or end titles that roll at the conclusion of a movie or other cinematic production.

How to Contact Potential Interviewees

You may write for some publication that will put you in touch with an interviewee, their management, or their representative. Such was the case with an interview I conducted with Scott Kirkland of The Crystal Method for *PopMatters*. You may have someone you know that is a potential interviewee, which is why so many books about Hollywood and its movies are written by people in Hollywood who already know all the people and have the connections. A friend of mine who lives about twenty minutes away has a band named Level 2.0. I conducted several interviews with him for various online publications. Author Leigh Rourks teaches at the same college as me. I conducted an interview with her, made two interviews from it, and sent one to *Aji*, a creative writing magazine that I read fiction and prose for, and *Route 7 Review*, a journal that has published an article and several reviews I wrote.

Sometimes someone gives you a tip or a referral. In the case of *The Fantastic Four*, much of the cast kept in touch and still knew one another. They often suggested someone else I should talk to and gave me contact information. Rebecca Staab (Susan Storm / The Invisible Girl), Jay Underwood (Johnny Storm / The Human Torch), Michael Bailey Smith (Ben Grimm), Carl Ciarfalio (The Thing) Alex Hyde-White (Reed Richards / Mister Fantastic), and Joseph Culp (Victor Von Doom / Doctor Doom) all stayed in touch and continue to see one another. Several of them recommended I talk to Mark Sikes who had made a documentary on *The Fantastic Four* titled *Doomed*. Mark Sikes put me in touch with a lot of the cast and crew. Some of them he either had not had a chance to interview for the documentary or they did not want to go on the record about the movie at that time. Directors seem to know everyone because they have to work with or have communication with virtually everyone involved in the film. Oley Sassone directed *The Fantastic Four* and he graciously put me in touch with several people he mentioned in the course of his interview including Mick Strawn and Everett Burrell. Mick Strawn offered to put me in touch with Peter Von Sholly. One strategy is to ask the interviewee if they know of someone else knowledgeable, useful, interesting, or good to talk to and if they have contact information for that person or those people. This way, you are always getting that next lead. The time to ask that question is usually near or at the end of the current interview since it is a forward-looking question and you are, in a sense, asking for a favor, an additional favor since they have already given you one favor by agreeing to the interview. Sometimes people wrap up a project and everyone goes their separate ways, but you never know who knows that one person you'd love to interview. Of course, the director, cast, crew, writers, and so forth may know other people connected to the movie you are writing about at the moment but they may also be able to connect you with people you may want to talk with in the future. According to the six degrees of separation theory, you are, at most, only six social connections away from anyone in the world.

Unofficial websites operated by fans are overrun with requests from other fans to put them in touch with the stars or pass messages along. Not only will they most likely not do this for you, they may not have the information to connect you even if they wanted to. Fan websites can have other interesting or useful information in their forums or link to or copies of articles and interviews, but do not depend on them for contact information.

Don't overlook the potential power of social media sites such as Twitter and Facebook—especially if the accounts are run by the potential interviewee themselves—to connect you.

Often, you will find an authorized website focused on a specific individual and run by them or their representatives. Often, the site contains an email contact feature or sometimes you will discover a directory and multiple email addresses for functions such as booking, or press/media inquiries; if there are multiple addresses listed, direct your message to the appropriate one and definitely not all of them. If there is a phone number, this is an especially good sign since publishing a phone number indicates the person is highly contactable. Nevertheless, first try email. Generally, if you are going to get a response, you will receive it within twenty-four to seventy-two hours. Some sites have someone else reading and responding to queries. William Shatner and John Saxon both had other people decline on their behalf. They did so cordially and the same day I sent the query. In quite a few cases, the individuals themselves responded to me directly. Other times, I never heard anything back. Why I don't know. My guess would be either the volume of emails a given person receives and/or excessive spam. If you do not receive a response on the first try, it is doubtful that you will on subsequent tries (I never have). Remember, these sites receive everything from princes offering huge sums of inheritance in exchange for personal banking information, children who want to talk about how much they love the movie, customers who have misdirected their questions or complaints about merchandise that may be sold on the site, students working on a report asking for help, super fans, the obsessed, the unhinged and deranged, the rambling, the literate, the semiliterate, the pre-literate, and anyone else capable of manipulating a keyboard or smartphone and pressing a button.

If attempting to contact someone via email, the most important step you can take to try to guarantee that your email gets read and considered is to develop a strong title in the subject line. The person looking through emails will not recognize your email address, so the first piece of information they will have is the subject line. The best phrase to use is "Interview Query." This states your business quickly and concisely. *Query* sounds more professional than *request*. If you have a book project contracted or in mind, you can also try something like "Book Interview (Subject of the Book or Focus of the Interview)." *Book* makes your request sound professional and serious (don't say you are professional; show you are professional). What do you want to interview the person about? Their role in a particular movie? Their strategy for matching socks? What, exactly? Letting them know the focus of the interview shows them that you are focused and either piques their interest or give them a chance to decline before either side invests any more time and effort. Listing the topic is important because perhaps your potential interviewee is tired of talking about your topic or has bad memories associated with it and doesn't want to discuss it. They can go ahead and refuse now. The reverse may be true. They may be tired of talking about topics a, b, and c but since you want to interview them about topics j and k, they are willing to consent to an interview. For *The Fantastic Four*, I used something like "Book Interview (The Fantastic Four / Roger Corman)." That sounds more unique and professional than "A Fan" or "Something to Ask."

The internet, of course, gives you other possibilities for contact. If you are interviewing television and movie cast and crew, you should be familiar with IMDB. Besides listing everyone who worked on the movie—even the uncredited—you can find contact information. You may find a website, an email address, a phone number, or other tip. You may get the name of a manager or agency that represents your person, but no further information. If so, you can look that information up. Following one clue/lead to the next is part of the process. IMDB also offers a pay feature called IMDbPro that may give you more information. When I interviewed Barry Schrader, he told me he had an IMDbPro membership and asked me if there was anyone else I was trying to contact. I told him Grace Zabriskie and Sid Haig. Grace Zabriski's contact information matched what was already on her website. Sid Haig's, however, listed the name of and contact information for his manager. I contacted his manager and that lead to an interview, probably one of his last. If you don't want to invest in a yearly or monthly membership, IMDbPro offers a thirty-day free trial. If you have a large project and have mapped out everyone you wanted or thought you might want to talk to, you could use the free trial to stock up on contact information for those names.

Going into your preferred search engine and typing someone's name along with the term "agent," "manager," "agency," or "public relations," may help you find a point of contact. If you are trying to contact bands or musicians, some of the details are different but the basic strategy is still the same. Generally, finding the name of the record label and manager is pretty easy. Amazon, Wikipedia, and the band's own site usually has that kind of information. If you are the kind of person like me who still buys physical media, the booklets that come with CDs and box sets are chock full of that sort of information. You can begin sleuthing it out from there. Don't overlook Bandcamp. I once used the contact feature and heard back from one of the founders of the band's record label (he agreed to line up an interview with the band once they were done making their current album). You never know who is on the other end of the computer. There are other bands on that label I might like to interview in the future, so I am definitely saving that email address.

Most of the music I review, I have to find myself. However, there are a few record labels that have me on email lists that send announcements, for example, when new music is close to coming out. Sometimes these emails have links to a new release and sometimes these emails say that recipients can request a copy of a particular new release. One such email was about a new Ministry album.

I requested the album and asked about interviewing a member of Ministry. I ended up talking with Sin Quirin and placing the album review on *Brutal Resonance*. Again, any sort of correspondence you receive—even a mass email sent to a mailing list—can contain an idea or a lead for an interview.

Every now and again, a potential interview may come to you. A member of a band named The Autumn Stones emailed me with a positive comment on a review I had written. I had never heard of them. We corresponded a bit and that turned into an interview with them for *COMA Music Magazine*. One of the members launched another project, Loveproof, and I interviewed them, too.

Besides helping put you in touch with an interviewee they worked with on the film or television show you are writing about, a current contact can put you in touch with someone who worked on another film or television show you might like to focus on. For example, I didn't get the Robert Englund interview by contacting his website. I tried using the contact button multiple times and never heard anything back (I don't know why, and I wasn't going to waste interview time asking why, although it's probably due to the reasons stated earlier). He was the last interview I conducted for the New World Pictures / Roger Corman project, but he was actually the first person I contacted for that collection. In between starting and finishing my part of those volumes of interviews, I began and finished an entirely different project, *The Fantastic Four* interviews. After I finished that, I realized that one of the people I interviewed had worked with Robert Englund, so I asked them if they could refer me to Englund. My contact knew someone on Facebook close to Englund and asked them to ask Englund. He said yes, so remember anyone you talk to in the interview chain—whether they are the actual interviewee or not—may be able to connect you, or help connect you, with someone else you want to interview.

Of course, not everyone can or will connect you to someone else. I had an idea for a separate project on a particular movie and one of the people I have interviewed was part of that movie. I asked them about connecting me with cast and crew from that movie. They did not get back to me directly, but forwarded my email to their publicist who did email and offered me a phone conversation to discuss the project. That person said they would talk to the manager of the person I interviewed. I never heard anything back. In between, I've been busy with other projects. The publicist was very nice, but I definitely picked up on the vibe that I might get better results by following a more formal protocol. If I were to go back to that project and pursue it further, I would contact my interviewee's manager directly with a professional query letter. If nothing else, I tested the idea a little and picked up another email address and phone number that could be of future use. Think of every interaction as practice, experience, and work towards building something else, even if you don't know what that something else is yet. If nothing else, you've made a decent impression on that person and you never know how or when your name may come up. Position and present yourself in such a way that people can speak positively of you should the opportunity arise.

When I was digging for interviewees for *Forsaken*, Stan Lee seemed like an obvious choice, and I wanted him to have not just a place but a voice in his own words in my book. Several people knew Stan Lee and agreed to contact him for me, but they didn't hear anything back. While I would have loved to talk with Stan Lee, it may have been better for the project that I was unable to. One of my interviewees told me Stan would probably not want to talk about the 1994 Fantastic Four film. I had heard Stan was not in great health. While I was working on *Forsaken*, an interview with him was published that confirmed Stan was not doing well (he passed before I finished the book). If I had spoken with him, I would probably have limited the scope to the origins of the Fantastic Four and I can't imagine that we would have talked for very long. A lot of issues and questions remained. Some people thought he should have been more of an advocate for *The Fantastic Four*. Some seemed to blame him for the movie never receiving a formal release. There was anger. Some wondered if he had seen the movie and, if so, what he thought of it. While researching for the collection, I discovered that Robert Ito wrote an article that coincided with the release of the 2005 big-budget *Fantastic Four* that explored the history of the 1994 *The Fantastic Four*. Stan Lee's responses suggest that he probably thought the purpose of the interview was to focus on the 2005 version. However, Ito focuses more on the 1994 version. Ito used a few quotes from the interview for his article, but the interview itself was never published . . . until I contacted him, asked him about it, asked for his permission to use it, and published it in my collection of interviews. So while I never got the opportunity to speak directly with Stan Lee, I did instead get a thorough interview with him about the 1994 film that was conducted when he was in better health, his knowledge of the film was fresher by more than a decade, and he was more open to discussing it. Bernd Eichinger who had the rights to make the 1994 movie and helped produce the first 2005 version and its sequel was also quoted in Ito's article. Eichinger was another important figure who didn't want to talk about the 1994 version. Ito also generously allowed me to use his interview for my book. If I had gotten a live interview with Stan, I would probably never have contacted Ito or thought about asking him for the Eichinger interview (Eichinger passed in 2011, years before I started the project). Both of these are extremely rare situations when someone literally hands an interview off to you.

However, the blue unicorn of interviews may be when you think you have found one person, but it is actually someone else—and yet both are useful. In the case of *Forsaken*, I very much wanted to talk with Chris Walker who was involved with the special effects for *The Fantastic Four*, but no one knew how to contact him. Heightening the mystery and my desire to talk to him, was my comparison of movie credits on IMDB between *The Fantastic Four* (1994) and *Fantastic Four* (2005)—yes, I read through all of the credits for both movies and compared them side-by-side. I was curious to see if there was anyone who had worked on *both* films. After all, Bernd Eichinger was involved with both. I found the same name in both sets of film credits: Chris Walker. I found a company Walker had worked for, emailed them, told them about the project, and asked if they could forward my email to him. They did and he responded from his personal email address, but he told me that although he was indeed Chris Walker and had worked on the 2005 *Fantastic Four* and its sequel, he was not the same Chris Walker who had worked on the 1994 version. There were two Chris Walkers who had both worked on Fantastic Four films. Incredible! This was too interesting not to include in some way, so I exchanged a few more emails with Walker, asked if I could compile them into a short interview, and he agreed (he also offered to put me in touch with people who had worked on those big-budget Fantastic Four films, good to know if I ever wanted to go in that direction).

However, I still had to locate the Chris Walker from 1994. I used the same techniques. By using his name, information from IMDB about companies he had worked for, and trying various search terms with information about him including Mr. Film, his animation studio which he sold and has since morphed into Modern Cartoons, I eventually located him. I found an email address at Modern Cartoons, which has a biography of him that does not mention *The Fantastic Four*. Apparently, he still receives mail there but emailed me from a different address belonging to a landscape architecture business where he currently works. I didn't know he was out of the movie business, so I would never have looked for him outside of that arena. Besides a great interview, he also gave me the cover image for *Forsaken*. You never know what will lead to what.

On that note, I should that mention that Punch Audio, Alex Hyde-White's audiobook company, created the audio version of *Forsaken*. Having played Reed Richards and a number of other roles, Hyde-White started getting into the production side of Hollywood. Truly, it is a small world after all.

How to Ask for an Interview

Generally speaking, the contact information you will find will be either an email address or a phone number. I suggest trying email first. It's less intrusive and by using email you have a chance to compose your query and say exactly what you want to say exactly the way you want to say it. Your email address should sound professional or at least neutral. Some variation of your name is perfectly acceptable: first name and last name, first initial and last name, initials and some series of numbers, and so on. Hotman4121@, superpsychochick69@, and Iamdeesheet@ are not acceptable. Similarly, avoid political or religious messaging in your email address as well as anything else potentially divisive or inflammatory. I don't know that the domain name is especially relevant. Gmail says, "current." Hotmail says, "not current." If you have something especially impressive, relevant, and with immediate brand recognition like harvard.edu that you can use as a domain name, then by all means use it to your advantage.

Think of this sort of as a job interview and you are applying for the role of interviewer. What's your experience? What are your skills and qualifications? Why should this person "hire" you and agree to an interview? Are you worth their time? How do you handle yourself? All those initial judgements will be made from first contact.

Once you have contact information, the next step is to compose a query letter. The letter should be concise and professional. After the salutation, I begin with what I am doing and what it is for, what I am asking for, other people I have interviewed or that are being interviewed for the project, any projects I have completed, any people I have interviewed within the same medium (film, music, and so forth), and a concluding comment.

Here is a basic template I have used.

*

Hello [first name last name]:

I am seeking an interview with you about your involvement with the unreleased Fantastic Four movie from 1994. I have a book contracted with BearManor Media on the film. So far I have completed interviews with Roger Corman (co-executive producer), Glenn Garland (co-associate producer and film editing), Craig J. Nevius (screenplay), Oley Sassone (director), Jay Underwood (the Human Torch), Carl Ciarfalio (the Thing), Joseph Culp (Doctor Doom), Rebecca Staab (the Invisible Girl), Michael Bailey Smith (Ben Grimm), Mark Sikes (casting assistant, producer of *Doomed: The Untold Story of Roger Corman's the Fantastic Four*), Kat Green (Alicia Masters), Alex Hyde-White (Mister Fantastic), Mick Strawn (production design), Pete Von Sholly (storyboard artist), Everett Burrell (special effects makeup), David Keith Miller (Trigorin, Doom henchman), the Wurst Brothers (soundtrack), John Vulich (special effects—from an unreleased video courtesy of Mark Sikes), Lloyd Kaufman, Chris Gore, Mark Parry (cinematographer), and Robert Alan Beuth (Dr. Hauptman).

I recently completed interviews with Sid Haig, Grace Zabriskie, Alex Hajdu, Durinda Wood, and Barry Schrader as part of another contracted book project. [as that project is now out I would list it including the title, press, and year of publication].

I hope to hear your perspective. Thank you for your consideration.

Best,
William Nesbitt

*

I generally reserve *dear* for family and close friends, so I often don't use *dear*, but I want to sound friendly so I use *hello*, which sounds a little more formal than *hi*. *Hey* just doesn't feel appropriate to me for a first-contact email. I then use the first and last name of the reader. Usually, I contact people directly. If I know I am contacting a manager or other intermediary, then I would begin instead with something like "I am seeking an interview with (blank) about (blank) and am hoping you will connect us." In the second sentence, I let the reader know where the interview will appear. If this is for a book, I name the press and use the word *contracted* to add validity to the project. Do not lie about this or anything else in your query. If the project is under review at a press, say so and state which press. If you don't have a contract and have not contacted a press yet, tell the reader which press or presses you plan to approach. Same thing with a magazine or website. If this is for a specific publication, name it. If you are hoping to place it with a specific publication or publications name it/them. If you have already interviewed specific people, list them. If you have any particularly impressive names and/or positions such as director you have interviewed, put them first. If you have interviews pending and/or people you plan to contact, list them also. It all lends validity, demonstrates that you have a blueprint, and establishes your credentials. If there are other people you have interviewed within the same genre, state their names; in a film query, it's irrelevant to name a musician I had talked to unless that person is either a huge name or I hadn't conducted many interviews and that's the best experience I could list. If you have other projects you have worked on, I would include those on another line.

I end by restating the request for the interview ("I hope to get your perspective") and thank them for their consideration. I close with my first name because it sounds more personal and in the first email I include my last name. I usually don't include Dr. or Ph.D.—unless I am contacting someone at a school, college, or university—because I think it is irrelevant at best and at worst risks sounding pompous, maybe even intimidating and/or out of touch. I might end with Professor of English and the place where I teach. Often, I mention I teach English. While I hardly think teaching English is a prerequisite for interviewing someone, sharing that information indicates that I am a professional and that I know something about writing. It also makes me stand out, which I think is an advantage. I want to appear capable, knowledgeable, experienced, and that I can take a project to completion. The way to convey that is to show it—not just say it—through concrete examples.

If you want to add in something else about appreciating the person's body of work or a specific film or album, there is nothing wrong with that, but keep it to a minimum. I think you should absolutely avoid saying you are a fan. Fans are important because they are consumers who spend money and they provide free advertising through word-of-mouth, social media, and so on, but lots of people are fans. *Fan* has also some connotations that you may not want attached to you and your request. Fans are obsessive. Fans want to be your friend and cling to you. Fans want to gush about how much your work means to their life. Fans want to get close to you, touch you, possess you. Fans can be weird. Fans can be scary. John Lennon autographed a copy of his album *Double Fantasy* for Mark

David Chapman six hours before Chapman shot and killed him. You do not want to give fans your contact information. *Fan* is short for *fanatic*. Assuming it is true, you can say you are a *scholar* of that person's work or that you have previously written something about it or studied it and give the specific instance (e.g., review, article, conference paper, a class, and so forth). Even mentioning having read a book, article, or review by or about your interviewee and naming something specific that stood out to you, indicates that you might be more than just a fan.

Keep your experiences relevant. I have some academic publications and some creative writing published, but I don't list those. If I do reference them, I sum them up in a single sentence. Just as if I were applying to read a paper on the economics of *The Merchant of Venice* for a Shakespeare conference panel, I don't know why it would matter to the conference or panel organizers that I interviewed Tom Shear of Assemblage 23 about his latest album. If there is some sort of a connection between two dissimilar experiences, you could try explaining the connection, but it's probably not worth the expenditure of words. Remember, people are busy.

I'd try to keep the whole query to 250 words or less. Do not beg.

Hearing Back

Most people, or their representatives, I hear back from within twenty-four to seventy-two hours. If you do not hear back from them within that timeframe, you are probably not going to ever hear back from them. I note the date of first contact in my spreadsheet. It is perfectly acceptable to let a week or two pass and then try again, especially if you are using the general contact function on their public webpage. However, I never heard back from anyone on subsequent tries. If you do not hear back from them, then that is a no. That silence is your answer. Assuming your request has not been jumbled in with spam and miscellaneous emails, whoever weeds through those emails has enough on their hands responding to the ones that absolutely require response and action. Generally, people simply do not or will not take the time to give you a quick "no thanks." You will get used to it and come to appreciate even the shortest, formulaic, and most impersonal of declinations because at least someone responded. That's another reason to find the name of a talent agency or manager representing the person you want to talk to: Sending the same request has a higher chance of being read and considered. Many people with be familiar with Big Star but fewer people will know the name or take the time to find the name of Big Star's management or public relations person. Sending requests to those types helps narrow and filter the stream your request is running through since the volume of correspondence will be less but simultaneously contain more serious offers and items of note, meaning all correspondence receives more attention.

Payment

I've never offered payment, and I've never had an interviewee ask for payment. I've never gotten into profit-sharing, percentages, points, guarantees, one-time payments, ongoing payments, or anything regarding money. I've had a few conversations with manager, agents, and public relations specialists and when the subject of money—as one person termed it "profit potential"—comes up, I already know where this is going. It's just a complication that I don't want to get into and can't afford. There is very little money in any of this for me; I figure over the course of my lifetime none of these projects will even provide a return equal to minimum wage for the hours I have put in. The upside about not being motivated by money is I take projects that look interesting and fun to me, and I don't have to depend on a project to support myself. I work with publications with which I have a good relationship and that appreciate my efforts since I am working for free. The only reason I can afford to do this is because it is a side hustle and not my primary source of income (teaching pays the bills, so that is my priority and I work side projects around my primary job, not the other way around). The world can be a small place and word travels, so I am also concerned about setting a precedent by paying for an interview.

What I can offer people is a chance to express themselves fully and an opportunity to promote themselves. I don't have to edit their words down to a small column or a one- or two-hundred-word box, and I'm not looking to dig out a sound bite or two. My understanding is that very few people get any kind of chance to look over, edit, add, or take out anything from their interview, so I also offer people some control over the final version. Finally, while I am primarily interested in interviewing and journalism as a way to uncover something new and get to the truth of someone's perspective and lived experience, I am well aware of the power of promotion through interviews and I am happy to aid that process whether it is talking about a new album that was just released, an upcoming book, a project looking for a home, or someone's side business. These things are relevant and people want to read about them; sometimes the major point of the interview is to talk about the new thing someone is doing. I have also offered to send a link or, at times, a print version of the final interview. While I am happy to do what I can to make someone satisfied with the final draft and to help promote them and their projects, I don't pay people to talk with them.

Increasingly, celebrities offer paid opportunities to video chat with them for a few minutes. That's not enough time for an interview. Trying to convert a casual interaction with a fan into an actual interview seems like an ambush. You could, perhaps, use that window of opportunity to ask them directly for a future interview. However, there is no guarantee that will even work. Also, if you can locate information about paid interactions, you may very well be able to find other avenues to present your interview request.

The One That Got Away (Or That I Finally Let Go)

The path from getting an interview agreement, time, and date to actually conducting the interview is not always direct. Delays, roadblocks, detours, and hassles can all be part of the terrain. Once, I was even stood up but eventually I got that interview.

I have only one experience with an interview someone agreed to and that was scheduled but never materialized. The interviewee was part of a rock band that charted in the American top ten a couple of decades ago. Since then, he has released some other projects. He was promoting the latest album with his current project, and a website I do some writing for asked me if I wanted to conduct an interview with this musician. I am very familiar with his earlier music, so my answer was an immediate "yes." The website emailed me some timeslots to choose from and I sent a few possible times that worked well for me. The musician's promoter responded that there were new days and times, and offered some new slots from a round of interviews that would take place a couple of weeks after the first round. I made some new choices. This time, I received confirmation of the day and time along with the musician's phone number. Once I've got that kind of information, I assume the interview is certain. I listened to the new album several times as preparation and worked on making questions. Looking at the timeslots, I could tell that interviews were scheduled in half-hour blocks. I carefully crafted sixteen questions.

At 3:07 the day of our scheduled interview, I received an email from the promoter that our 4:30 interview would be postponed and I was told to check back tomorrow (to be fair, the promoter may have given me almost as much notice as the musician had given him). I checked back the next day and heard nothing in return. I sent a final email two weeks later and also got no response. I decided there was little point in sending another email. A couple of weeks later, I was looking at the musician's webpage, and saw an email address for his publicist. I contacted him and made no reference to my prior attempts as I didn't think that would help me.

Not expecting much, I kept it short and wrote the following email.

*

Hello [blank]:

I am seeking an interview with [name]. I have reviews, interviews, and articles with *The Rockpit, Sleaze Roxx, PopMatters, Brutal Resonance, ReGen,* and *Coma* among others. Complete publications list available upon request. I am a professor of English at Beacon College. [yes, I know earlier I wrote that I normally don't mention being a college professor, but for whatever reason, I did so this time.]

Thank you for your consideration.

Best,
William Nesbitt

*

Somewhat surprisingly, the publicist thanked me for reaching out and asked me to provide links to samples of my work. I was told that they would make a determination after reviewing those materials. That took about forty-five minutes to create since I keep screenshots and a running list of publications, but not with links. I produced something resembling the list in the "Make and Maintain a Portfolio" section of this book. After the interview listings with links, I included a bulleted list—sans links—with all of the online reviews and articles I have written, and I offered to send any additional information they wanted. The publicist thanked me for the information, complimented me on my publications, told me when the musician preferred to do interviews, and asked about what format we would use to conduct the interview. So far, so good. I thanked the publicist for the kind words, talked about my availability, suggested we do the interview over the phone, and thanked the publicist for his help coordinating everything. Five days later, I got a response back stating that the publicist spoke to the musician's wife and she recommended that I speak with a specific member of the band (whose name I won't share) who is the musician's right-hand man, working right along with the musician. I am further informed that the musician is fully booked. Hmmmm . . . I find this a bit suspect. Time to dig deeper.

Before I give an answer, I research the right-hand man. While he is a member of the musician's band, the right-hand man is not listed on or credited with working on any of the musician's records. As best I can tell, he seems to be what we would call a "touring member"—someone who doesn't write music but whose job is to reproduce live what someone else has written and played on the records. At the time of the proposed interview, the right-hand man was around twenty-one, so his window of opportunity as the musician's right-hand man would had to have begun pretty recently. In the midst of my research, I find a collection of pictures with the right-hand man and the musician's daughter. It's immediately obvious that the right-hand man and the musician's daughter are in a romantic relationship. Captions I find with various photos of the two of them confirm this with phrases like "love of my life."

Well, there are two ways to think about this. The publicist was very polite and easy to deal with. The musician was unavailable for whatever reason, and perhaps the publicist was trying to offer me what he could. Maybe the right-hand man did a lot of work behind the scenes or had recently moved into a more collaborative role and formal credit did not or had not yet begun to reflect that (all of this doubtful, I think, but possible). I could still have an interview. Maybe the right-hand man would go on to do more since he has decades left in his career and I could say, "I interviewed him before he did . . . ." I also considered the possibility that if I interviewed the right-hand man, it might help position me for a subsequent interview with the musician. The other way to think about it is I have gotten the runaround from two people, I would have to make almost all new questions as only two of the sixteen were transferable (and generating new questions for someone with such limited experience would be a challenge), I was quite possibly being blatantly lied to about the right-hand man's role, and I went from interviewing the musician, who had a long career and lots of albums, to the musician's daughter's boyfriend, who was at the beginning of his but had no records yet. If I was just getting started with interviewing and needed the experience, didn't have other projects I was working on, was really fascinated with this current phrase of the musician's career, or was really determined to get an interview with the musician and saw this as a potential stepping stone, then maybe I'd have taken the offer. Two people I discussed this episode with separately—one in the music business and one not—each independently used the word *disrespected* to describe how they thought I was treated. This is the email I sent to the publicist.

*

Hello [blank]:

Thanks for your help with everything and I appreciate the possibility of an alternative interview with [new person]. However, all of the time I have put into preparing questions and other such activity to get ready for this interview was directed towards [original person].

Best,
William

*

I did not receive a response. I'm not quite sure if I'd call it a bait-and-switch but it feels similar to that, even if it didn't start that way. The situation could be as simple as people get busy, they get overbooked, and they have to prioritize. What really happened is unknown to me. I can speculate, but the bottom line is that three times the situation looked like it was going one way (up) and then it went another way (down). The musician friend I talked to was surprised I didn't get into it more with the publicist when I passed on the interview and call the publicist out on it. I told him that I didn't think there was a need for that, I had already put enough time into the whole fiasco that I wasn't going to get back, and I didn't know if I might cross paths again with him or someone he knows, so I didn't want to potentially burn a bridge. In this case, I doubt the publicist had much, if anything, to do with the musician backing out—don't kill the messenger. Plus, I told my friend that the publicist isn't dumb. He'll know what I am really saying in my diplomatic version, which is "This doesn't make sense. I'm not sinking more time into it. I'm done. 'Preciate yah. Pass!" My musician friend told me that when I got that first email right before the scheduled interview telling me that the interview was going to be postponed, I should have acted as if I never received that email and called anyway. If I had known what was going to happen, I might have done that.

My musician friend still thinks I should just call the musician up out of the blue and try to get the interview, but I decided against that; I just don't feel comfortable with the idea. I don't know how much the musician knew or remembers about any of this (quite likely nothing). I doubt the musician will just take an out-of-the-blue call with someone he doesn't know, take me at my word that I have experience and can place the interview with a publication, and then talk with me for at least ten minutes. I can't imagine the musician not asking how I got his number and why I am calling him. What do I say? "You owe me an interview?" "You cut out on multiple interviews with me, but I'm going to ignore that and push you into it anyway?" I can't expect that I can just call with no notice or introduction, start asking questions, and the person on the other end will just go along with it. I definitely can't demand an interview. Yes, I was led on several wild goose chases, but I don't think that entitles me to anything from him or anyone else. I appreciate the ear, support, and brainstorming from my musician friend, but that's not an option for me. Maybe someone with a different style or personality could pull that off. If I used the musician's personal phone number for anything, it would be to text him and try to start a conversation about having an interview. Even that seems like it could be too presumptuous, bordering on rude.

Should I ever interview the musician, I think it needs to happen with his agreement, and I can't see any advantage in referencing this saga (another reason I am not sharing names). I place "or finally let go" in the parentheses of this section heading because I suppose I could take a break and try again or try contacting someone else in his camp since I never heard a total refusal, but it's not worth it to me at this time.

I share this whole experience for three reasons. First, that you, dear reader, have a sense of how you can get strung around. I think it's always good to prepare for a scheduled interview assuming that it will indeed happen, but it's also good to remember there is no guarantee you will get a reward for your time and energy. Like all investments, you give the resources before getting the return. Two, the experience is not a total waste. Besides learning from it, I have a story to share in these pages that might benefit you. Three, this is not the only situation in my life when someone wouldn't come out and say, "no" but they wouldn't do whatever they said they would do. You have to analyze the overall picture, see how it makes you feel outside of the heat of an immediate emotional reaction, and find that cutoff point for yourself. You, your peace of mind, and your self-esteem matter more than any interview. Other good things will come.

Scheduling Interviews

If you are fortunate enough to receive an acceptance and secure the interview, usually there will be some mention of scheduling it. You will be given some general timeframes and/or you will be asked to give some general timeframes. You should try to present as open a schedule on your part as you possibly can. Although most interviews will occur Monday through Friday, you should state your availability, of lack thereof, on weekends. If you have any unique but set-in-stone items in your schedule such as a trip, an event, or another interview already scheduled that require you to blackout a certain block of time, state that upfront. Generally, the other party will offer you a time and day for the interview and schedule it within a few days or weeks. It can be longer. For example, your interviewee may be shooting on location and prefers to return home before proceeding.

Other times, you will get consent for the interview, but cannot get it scheduled. This can feel maddening. If you receive a flat no or a yes and schedule the interview, then you know where you stand. The yes without a time and date puts you in a state of limbo. What to do?

I've generally got something else to focus on whether it is another interview, writing project, or items related to work and teaching, so I just move forward with something else and circle back later. I have rarely had someone agree to an interview and later renege. I take *no* to mean no and do not press further. However, if you say yes, I may hound you forever until you either give me the interview or reverse your offer. Patience is called for. My strategy is to check back about once a month and use polite persistence. *Polite persistence*. Both words are equally important. To get the interview, sometimes you must persist, but you must always be polite.

I'll give an example. We'll refer to the person in this example as "Film Person." I contacted them with an initial request and heard back from them about fifteen hours later. Pretty good! Film Person said they were wrapping up on a show, would be back in town in a week, and then maybe we could find a good time for both of us. So far, so good. I gave it ten days and wrote the following message.

*

Dear Film Person: [note: In this case, I used *dear* with them because they used *dear* with me.]

I hope your trip went well. If you any ideas for when we might be able to talk, please let me know.

Best,
William

*

Something short and to the point is fine. I wanted to begin with something friendly and then the second sentence is just a short reminder. Not enough time has elapsed that I figured I needed to remind the reader about who I am and what we talked about. I received a response that same day asking if the middle of the following month—about three weeks from the date of the response—would be good. Film Person also explained that they had a personal situation involving a sick family member and apologized for life interfering.

*

Dear Film Person:

I am sorry to hear that you have sickness in your family. I wish for the most positive prognosis and a speedy recovery. The quote has been attributed to various people, but it says, "life is what happens when you're busy making other plans." The middle of next month, September, will work fine for me. In the meantime, I will be thinking positive thoughts for your family member and you.

Best,
William

*

I was very sorry to hear of the ill family member. It's a reminder that we all have personal lives and have the same problems. No one is exempt. This email calls for a caring and concerned tone. I framed the majority of the email around their personal situation and devoted just a single sentence to the matter of the interview. I waited until the 17th, just after the middle of September and followed up.

*

Dear Film Person:

I just thought that I would check in with you and see if life has calmed down enough for us to set up the interview. I hope everything is better and going well for you.

Best,
William

*

Same idea—short and to the point while still being polite with an acknowledgement of and concern for the personal situation coupled with a reminder about the interview. Empathize and emphasize. Just short of five weeks later, I sent this email.

*

Dear Film Person:

I just thought that I would check in with you and see if life has calmed down enough for us to set up the interview. I hope everything is better and going well for you.

Best,
William

*

Again, same idea—short message (the same message), expressing concern, and with something about the interview embedded. They sent a response the same day letting me know that they would be hearing something in a couple of days regarding the sick family member and giving me a specific date two weeks from now when they thought they would be ready to talk. That date came and went. Twenty days later, I sent the same email as above. Again, I received a response the same day. There was no update about the family member or our interview, but Film Person asked whether or not I had spoken with a specific cast member they named. I responded that I had previously tried to contact that person through their talent agency but had not received a response. That was late October and I let it rest until next year.

A little over five months later, I used what I call The Option of Last Resort. Essentially, this is when you try one final time to get the interview and let the interviewee know this is the last time you are going to try. This is the Hail Mary, the push forward of all the poker chips, the final bullet, the swing for the fences. This is when you have tried everything else. This isn't for someone who has been dragging their heels a little and a week has passed. In this situation, over eight months elapsed between my first contact and my final attempt. Sometimes people need deadlines and sometimes they need final deadlines. You want to be pleasant about the whole thing—again, no one owes you anything even if they have previously consented—but clear. Also, do not bluff. Be fully prepared to not ask again, to not get the interview, to not contact the person again, and to completely write it off. The Option of Last Resort calls for a different approach.

*

Hello Film Person: [note: Yep, looks like I dropped *dear*.]

I thought I would try one final time before giving up on getting an interview from you. We're pretty full with respondents and are good on material (we even got an interview from [name of Really Big Star]). I just did an interview with Big Star, which is my fourth interview, so I have plenty also. However, I'd love to get you in there, especially because [insert really compelling reason about why their experience is unique and important]. One of the interviews we have is just 600 words, so something relatively short would be fine. I talked with Big Star for about 20 minutes and that gave me plenty of material (not far from 2,000 words).

There are three options:

1. I can email you the questions and you can complete them. I can proof and edit from there.
2. You can record yourself, send it to me, and I can do the transcription.
3. I can talk with you via phone, record, and transcribe.

Please let me know. I'd really love to get your perspective. Hope all is well for you.

Best,
William

*

The intent with that letter is to convey a handful of key points to the interviewee:

A. This is my last attempt to get your interview.
B. I don't have to have your interview.
C. But I still want your interview.
D. This other person who is equal or above you in stature thinks this project is the real deal. Don't you want to be of the Cool Kids, too?
E. Your interview can be really short.
F. There are various ways to do the interview, so here are some convenient options.

Points D and F are important because they let the interviewee know that this doesn't have to be something long and they have a choice about how they want to do it. The idea is to emphasize how easy and convenient the interview can be. Make it sound as easy as possible. Easy, easy, easy.

I got a response back a day later informing me that Film Person wanted to ask me a few questions. Not exactly what I had hoped for, but a pulse had returned. I said, "Sure! Let me know how you want to proceed with that." Two days later, I followed up with "Still hoping to hear back from you . . . ." A day later they wanted to know the intended audience for the collection of interviews and was this to be an objective or sensational interview. Those are fair questions, though I wondered why I was getting them at this point. Was Film Person thinking about this interview more seriously, was this a stall tactic, or something else? I knew two things: It didn't matter what the intent was and I felt that how I answered these questions might be a factor in whether I ultimately ever got this interview or not. I had to think about this and be careful. The truth was, "Say whatever you like, and I'll figure it out" but I thought needed to respond with a little more finesse. This is what I came up with.

*

Dear Film Person:

I see it as for Corman fans, science fiction fans, and fans of a particular New World Pictures movie or movies. Additionally, there are people who may be interested in the career of the interviewee and will find it interesting to hear him or her talk about a time in their career that we may not have heard as much about.

If I had to pick between vanilla and tell-all, I think I would say it will probably lean more toward vanilla. Some people seem to hold Roger in nothing but high regard and that is fine. Others have had a sort of acknowledgment and perhaps appreciation for what being associated with his films have done for their career while also pointing out the low pay, incredibly tight deadlines, and other difficulties they faced in getting their part of the film done. I appreciate and welcome that perspective as well.

When I first contacted you, I made a list of questions. Since that time, I have made some changes, edited, subtracted, deleted, and so on. My idea for this interview is to take those questions, look at them with fresh eyes, and cut them down for a final list since some may be redundant (I can trim it down to just five to ten questions if that is all the time you have). Right now, I am including that larger list as an attachment because I think that may help show you my thoughts about the book and your interview.

Best,
William

*

In other words, "I'll take whatever you'll give me." I decided to sound as if I leaned more toward the harmless than the sensational simply because I figured Film Person would be more likely to speak with me. I also made room for a more dissatisfied or upset viewpoint by acknowledging I have talked with folks who shared memories of a blunter and less romantic nature. I also wanted Film Person to know I had gone to the effort to put together a list of questions and I figured these would be helpful in showing my commitment to the interview as well as providing a sort of roadmap for where we might go. Again, I put in a reminder that I would be happy with whatever time I could get.

Film Person informed me that they had located a copy of the movie, would watch it, and be in touch with me the following day. The following day I received an email asking me to call so we could talk. Luckily, I check email very, very frequently. Over eight months later and I was finally going to get the interview! That, however, was only part of the process as I will discuss when we pick up back up with the story in the next section.

Check Your Spam

You probably don't check your spam because, well, it's your spam. For years, I didn't check mine either. Then, I was corresponding about some edits with the interviewee I discussed in the previous section, and, suddenly, I stopped hearing from them. I thought that was odd. Five days later, I sent Film Person an email and they told me that they emailed me days ago and heard nothing back. This prompted me to check my spam folder and upon doing so and finding their emails, I wrote: "I just checked my spam folder and indeed there are three messages from you. My apologies. I marked those 'not spam' and that should not happen again. I will diligently check my spam from now on, though. Strange. That shouldn't happen with someone I am communicating regularly with." We resumed communication. I don't think Film Person held it against me, but I don't think I impressed them either.

However, I learned my lesson and while that never happened again with Film Person, it was not the last time I found messages in my spam folder from an interviewee. To this day, I check my spam every day. Prior to that diverted correspondence, I contacted other potential interviewees. As I have said, rather than respond with a "no," folks often just don't respond at all. I had assumed that lack of response indicated a refusal. What if somewhere in that neglected folder was a "yes" or some other response that might have led to a yes, but it just went to my spam folder unseen, unread, and eventually lost as spam folders periodically self-purge? This is without speculating about all the other potentially relevant and interesting communications I may have missed over the almost two decades I've had that particular email account. Well, as with all things in the past, I can't worry about what has already happened, especially if I don't know about it. Missed opportunities, phantom chances, and the ghosts of unknown choices can haunt us. I can't fret too much about what I don't know about. All I can do is take what I do know about the past, learn from it, and try to make better decisions now that I have better and/or more information. So, to repeat the first three words of this paragraph: Check your spam. Check. Your. Spam.

How Long Will the Interview Last?

Remember that good interviews do not necessarily have to be long interviews, but that brings up the question of how much time you need to conduct an interview. Thirty minutes seems to be a pretty good standard. If I need to include an amount time during the process of setting up the interview, I say around thirty minutes but I always say that even fifteen minutes will probably do. Ten is the absolute minimum I would attempt and for that to work, both sides must be focused and hit the ground running. I don't think I've ever had anything run shorter than fifteen minutes, though I have had two interviews that went well over three hours. For that reason, I suggest not assuming that the interview will only be thirty minutes. If your interviewee is giving interviews as part of a media push promoting a new product and you have seen a signup list or been offered specific times on specific dates, then there probably is a strict schedule they are adhering to. Since you may also be one of many interviews that day and everybody is human and gets tired, don't expect to get additional time.

In a couple of instances, I had more than one interview scheduled and I always left at least three hours between them, if for no other reason than to give me a chance to take a break, let the dogs out, stretch my legs, and take care of other necessary life tasks. I think it's best to get the interview as soon as you can. When offered a choice between sooner and later, I always take the soonest opportunity. People forget dates, get busy, plans change, life happens—all sort of events can occur so I believe in getting the interview while you can. I have also had people I have been trying to schedule an interview with suddenly tell me they can talk while they are driving or at dinner. If it's good for them, then it's good for me. As long as I am not teaching a class or driving—kind of hard to read questions and keep track of everything as the interviewer—I can do it. There have been a few times I have been working on nailing down an interview and I have kept a recorder and a set of questions with me just in case. I've never had it happen, but I would hate to lose a good interview opportunity because I was out and about and unprepared.

Yes, it may not seem fair to say you should be prepared to drop everything you are doing with little to no notice, find someplace to talk on the phone such as a park or the interior of your parked car in a random parking lot, and have questions and recording equipment to conduct an interview, but it's been worth it to me to make sure I don't get caught off guard and lose an opportunity. The window may open without warning and only once.

How Much and What Kind of Research Should You Do Beforehand?

You should always do your research in order to be prepared, perform due diligence, and show respect. You may not be familiar with every facet of someone's career or remember every detail, but people can figure out very quickly if you have some idea of their work or not, and they will often respond accordingly. If someone has a compact body of work—one album, one book, or one movie—that's pretty easy. You listen to, read, or watch whatever that thing is. If they have more output than that, then you may have to pick and choose unless you are some sort of scholar or super-fan of their work. Even then, it's good to review as most of us do not have a photographic memory. For example, I saw most of the original episodes of *Dallas* as a child when they aired and have caught some now and again on cable, but I hardly feel that would be recent enough to interview someone from the program. Seeing a preview of a movie, having read a novel ten years ago, reading a review, knowing a couple of songs off the radio—these are all better than nothing, but you need to have recent and in-depth familiarity with someone's output.

If you really have to cram and give yourself a crash course in someone's filmography, I recommend reading detailed summaries, watching previews on YouTube, and watching clips and/or key scenes. Music is even easier to find, and—unlike watching a film or television show—you can listen to it while engaged in other activities, if you are pushed for time. Most albums are around an hour long. Reading is the hardest of these three mediums to cut corners on. You will either have to sit down and do it or find an audio version. Remember, any summary cuts out details. The plot may be the foundation, but flavor comes from details.

Even if the interview concerns a particular work, knowing about other items the interviewee has been involved in can help you generate questions, make connections, and understand the particular piece the interview will focus on. When I interviewed Scott Kirkland about The Crystal Method's latest record, *The Trip Home*, their record label gave me access to the whole six-album catalog. I try to interview people whose work I like or think is interesting, so I enjoyed listening to The Crystal Method's entire catalog and jotting down notes and observations as I listened. Since I planned to spend the majority—but not all—of the questions on the newest record, I gave that my full attention and listened to it multiple times.

If I don't have time to review everything or the materials are not available—though with YouTube, there's not much excuse—I try to at least listen to the current album. When I interviewed Sin Quirin of Ministry, I knew we would have a maximum of twenty-five minutes and that I was supposed to focus on the new interview and upcoming tour. I already had some familiarity with their music from years of listening to 1992's *Psalm 69,* which was their "big" record, and I had seen them live, so given the tight focus and limited time, I asked the label for a copy of the new record, listened to it multiple times, and thought that would be enough preparation, which it was. I would not have time beforehand to listen to and digest thirteen albums, and Quirin and I would not have time to talk about them. The label also sent me a link to a video interview Sin had recently done. I made sure to watch that very closely as I figured I would be expected to be familiar with the content. It's similar to when a teacher writes something on the board, screen shares something, or puts it in the directions. Generally, that means it's important and you need to pay attention.

Books become a little trickier. I can't really read while I am doing something else, unless I am waiting for something or someone. When I interviewed Leigh Rourks, she had one book of short stories out, so that made it pretty easy. Her website has some of these stories along with a few essays and poems. I read all of it and made a bulleted outline of a few topics or themes I saw in them. Each bullet point was just a word or a short phrase, but this helped me think of the overall scope of her writing.

Films and television shows can become complicated. Writers don't generally have guest spots or cameos in books. Musicians sometimes do, but generally that is not what they are known for. Actors often have smaller parts, walk-on roles, and cameos that have rich stories behind them. Also, writers and musicians don't always compete and audition in the same way or to the same extent actors do for their spots. Often there are stories there in those gave-it-a-try, almost-happened, didn't-quite-work-out, was-offered-the-part-and-turned-it-down experiences. For example, Robert Englund has been asked/hounded/harassed about his not-quite-an-audition for *Star Wars*. I asked him about this experience at the end of an interview about New World Pictures, Roger Corman, and *Galaxy of Terror*. I ended up making an entirely separate interview out of that (more about that later). Actors and film people often have an entire secret or at least lesser-known history of missed or refused roles that chart an entirely alternate history that never happened. You often won't find out about this kind of stuff unless you actively look for it by researching.

Researching for film and television generally means finding out what that person was in or worked on. IMDB is a great source and is often more complete than Wikipedia (often people's first choice).

When it comes to film folks, I try to be aware of their major work. In the case of the New World Pictures / Roger Corman project, most of the people I talked to had only worked on one or two of his films. I read a little about other productions my interviewees had been involved in, but I drilled down on the NWP / Corman work. Basically, I focused on *Galaxy of Terror*, *Battle Beyond the Stars*, and *Death Race 2000*. I bought editions of each with special features. Besides watching the films multiple times in their entirety, I also watched all of the special features, especially any conversation with my interviewee. I watched all of the special features because I didn't know what might help me think of a question or when someone I wanted to interview might be mentioned by someone else. Besides, the general research is valuable, there is some interesting information in there, and if you specifically reference those bonus features in your interview, those references demonstrate your preparation. If it's available, get a copy of the script/screenplay. That can be using for clarifying lines of dialogue. Sometimes you can find it in the special features of a film, sometimes people have typed or scanned it and placed it on online, often in PDF format, and sometimes you can purchase reproductions for sale online at places like eBay.

I was extremely lucky in the case of *The Fantastic Four*. I had secured an interview—through Mark Sikes—with Craig J. Nevius who wrote the screenplay. I had been searching for an online or print copy, any copy, of the script and came across one on Amazon for $10. I received it before the interview, so I had a chance to look through it. It was very different in key places from the final version.

When I talked with Craig, I discovered this was a very early draft with some dramatic scenes and more serious content that had been cut, probably for issues of budget and pacing. It's an early record of a noticeably different version of the movie. Given the condition it's in, I think it is not a reproduction but an authentic draft. I'm sure it's worth more than what I paid for it, but besides being a cool and special item of memorabilia, it really helped inform my interview with Nevius. Reading that script showed him that I had done my homework and I was able to ask him some unique questions about what his intention was with certain things he had written and why some of those scenes never appeared. He had a collection of screenplays also, but did not have them readily available for reference. However, when I started reading lines and text to him, he immediately remembered and often could finish the sentences without help. Other times, when he was trying to remember something, I could flip through and quickly locate the information for him. What an excellent resource that turned out to be.

To get ready for the folks from New World Pictures, I read Corman's entire *How I Made a Hundred Movies in Hollywood and Never Lost a Dime*, which chronicles his life and focuses heavily on the New World Pictures era. Other than individual movies, this source would be the most useful to me as it gave me an overview of all the actors and films presented as a single narrative. *How I Made a Hundred Movies in Hollywood and Never Lost a Dime* helped with every interview for the project because it was relevant to every person I talked with. When I interviewed Corman for *The Fantastic Four* project, I quoted a specific line from the book, identified the book, and asked a question based on it. I found an inexpensive, used copy. Same with my Fantastic Four project. The *Doomed* documentary, which focuses on the Fantastic Four, and *The Fantastic Four* film were my two principal sources. For multi-interview projects, try to find these types of foundational sources that will help you with every interview and give you the most value for your time and money.

Often, you will have to supply your own source materials as I did with Corman's book and all of the NWP movies I watched. Consider it part of the price of interviewing, though you can often find lots of primary and secondary material online for free legally or through a service you already pay for such as cable and streaming accounts. You never know what your local library might have.

If your interviewee has a website, familiarize yourself with its contents and materials. You may find links to useful articles, reviews, and interviews. Sometimes there will be original content unique to the website itself. While it would be strange to announce and catalog what you did in preparation for the interview, that materials review should be obvious in your questions and exchanges. You don't want to look like uniformed. For example, when I was first trying to get an interview with Robert Englund, a friend of mine suggested I ask him what he thinks of the 2010 *A Nightmare on Elm Street* remake.

While at first that might seem like a good question, it's not for several reasons. My interview with Englund would focus on *Galaxy of Terror* since it would be part of a larger collection of interviews focused on New World Pictures. That's the sort of question I might ask at the end of the interview if I was curious and interested in the remake, which I'm not.

If I went outside of the NWP / Corman / *Galaxy of Terror* area, I'd ask about something I am more interested in such as *Star Wars*, which I am interested in and which I did ask about at the end. However, the main reason I didn't ask about the remake is that Englund's webpage has a FAQ with several questions about the remake, including "What did you think of the remake?" Englund is very gracious and I have little doubt that he would have answered the question, but asking it would have signaled that I had failed to perform even a basic review of his website. The exception to this would be if I referenced his answer and built a question off of that. However, even if I did that it would be even better to connect that to the main topics of Roger Corman, New World Pictures, or *Galaxy of Terror*, which is what I did. I figured Freddy Krueger would come up since that is Englund's signature role. He touched on the role a few times without my influence. The question I eventually asked was "In that doppelganger sequence in *Galaxy of Terror*, the evil Ranger holds a knife, flashes a wide, deranged smile, and slashes at the good Ranger. Did any of that carry forward to the Freddy Krueger character?" With that question, there is a clear connection between a specific scene in *Galaxy of Terror* and Freddy Krueger.

Though they may not remember every detail, people are familiar with their own careers and will be able to tell pretty quickly if you are, too. If you can't go deep with the questions, they probably won't go deep with the answers. Just knowing someone had a role in that movie or played in this band or wrote a story called "Fill in the

Blank" is not nearly enough. Stock questions will receive stock answers. Questions that have been asked before will receive answers we've already heard, seen, or read—what's the point?

People who have been interviewed a lot get asked the same questions. What kind of answer do they give to the same question? The same answer. Because they have been asked the same questions, they often have developed a standard answer. What happens when they get asked the same question and they have the same answer ready? They get bored. They switch into autopilot. The interview becomes rote. All of that comes through. If you want new and exciting answers, surprise your interviewee with fresh and engaging questions. That gets them interested and it short circuits that mental script they have developed and rehearsed from being asked the same questions over and over and over again. Besides reviewing the basic biography and relevant work (e.g., movie, music, book), the most important preparation is to read other interviews with your person. Depending on whom you are talking to, tracking down and reading all of their interviews may not be feasible, but you should read at least some. You may use one of the answers to generate your own follow-up question. You may see multiple interviews asking variations of the same question. Avoid asking those questions.

Creating Questions

Remember, that you do not want to just "wing it." If you don't have questions prepared, it's like shooting a film without a script or recording an album with no songs written. Even if you are comfortable talking with new people and good at extemporaneous speaking, everyone can get off track and talking to Big Deal Star can bring out the nerves more than you might anticipate.

So you've done your research for the interview. This means you have done some reading about your interviewee and their career. You've consumed, reviewed, or at least familiarized yourself with their output—or at a minimum their most significant productions—especially anything your interview will focus on, and you're read or watched some of the interviews that have already been conducted with your interviewee. Now, it's time to start drafting and putting together questions. In the case of the New World Pictures interviews, I prepared a template for all of the interviews. I tweaked that template over the course of the project and customized it for each particular interview. This is what I developed for Grace Zabriskie.

*

1. Let's begin with some background about yourself. How did you get started working on movies and television?
2. Did you read for the part? How long did it last? What was that meeting like?
3. How and when were you actually offered the part?
4. Was it always clear in your mind and everyone else's that you would play the part of Captain Trantor?
5. What recollections do you have about making *Galaxy of Terror* and of Roger Corman?
6. How much direction was there?
7. Was there a sense of trying to complete the film as quickly as possible?
8. Corman is a big fan of cost-cutting and we know *Galaxy of Terror* used recycled movie props and whatever else the crew could salvage. Besides using McDonald's Styrofoam containers as props and possibly renting the site out to a

German watch company, any other specific memories of things that were done to save money?

9. By the time of the film's release, you had about three years under your belt in movies and television and went on to perform in many, many other films and shows. How does *Galaxy of Terror* parallel or detour from those experiences?

10. What did you learn from being in *Galaxy of Terror*?

11. Did you ever have an opportunity to teach or suggest anything to anyone involved with *Galaxy of Terror*?

12. How did *Galaxy of Terror* influence your subsequent career?

13. Any connections between Captain Trantor and any of the other characters that you have portrayed?

14. As the crew lifts off for Morganthus, Captain Trantor only gives them thirty seconds to get buckled for takeoff, explaining that "seconds wasted here could be costing lives on Morganthus." Just as the crew have caught their breath, she proclaims, "if we have to get there at all, we might as well get there fast" and launches them into a hyper-jump. What's the rush? In the extras, you speak of Trantor's need "to assert her own authority."

15. Ultimately, Trantor catches fire and is burned alive in the airlock. What did you think about her demise?

16. What's it like being a woman making movies in the 1980s?

17. What did you and do you think about the maggot sex scene?

18. In the extras, director Bruce D. Clark says that "the part she had was not well-written" and the character had "some pretty dreadful lines." What do you think?

19. There are some memorable lines your character spoke. Can you tell us what these three lines mean? "An oxer in a breather bar," "Fame is the food that dead men eat," and "the master sends meat, but the devil sends cooks."

20. *Galaxy of Terror* was the only film you made with Corman. Why?

21. How did you think *Galaxy of Terror* would end up doing in the box office?

22. What did you think *Galaxy of Terror* would do for your own career?

23. What did you think critics would think of *Galaxy of Terror*?

24. The booklet included with *Galaxy of Terror* states that it has been listed in the top 50 worst movies of all time. Is this fair?

25. You said that "this has cult classic written all over it." What are the trademarks of a cult classic and how does *Galaxy of Terror* fulfill them?
26. Does the film have a message?
27. You said "the movie will be remembered many years for a number of things." What are the things you remember about *Galaxy of Terror*?

*

Most of these questions fall within several categories, with some overlap. Some questions I could use again verbatim. With some, all I had to do was add or delete the names of movies or characters and I could use them multiple times almost verbatim. The rest are specific to the actor or character. Nine takes a little more modification and sixteen is specific to women, but those are potentially reusable. Seeing the similarities and differences among answers from interviewees who are asked the same question can be illuminating, so don't be afraid to ask different people the same question. If you are concerned about using the same question with multiple people, you can always rephrase the question so that it reads differently. Questions that quote the actor, the movie, and/or any extra features from the movies help lend a sense of personalization to the interview and demonstrate that you have done some preparation. Question eight came from reading the booklet included with *Galaxy of Terror*.

You will see a similar pattern with the final list of questions I prepared for Oley Sassone, director of *The Fantastic Four*. However, this is the initial list.

*

1. How did you find you way to *The Fantastic Four*?
2. What recollections do you have about making *The Fantastic Four*?
3. What was co-executive producer Roger Corman's role?
4. Any encounters with Roger Corman or memories related to him?
5. What challenges or limitations did you experience while making the film?
6. Why was the film never released?
7. Referring to the film's cancellation Michael Bailey Smith (Ben Grimm) said, "It's like knowing you had the winning

lottery ticket and then lost it in the laundry." How big did you think the film was going to be?

8. What did you learn from working on *The Fantastic Four*?

9. Does the movie have a message?

10. What have you been up to since making *The Fantastic Four*? Other than being in the documentary *Doomed: The Untold Story of Roger Corman's The Fantastic Four* (2015), any more films or television programs related to comic books or Marvel?

11. Please complete this sentence "*The Fantastic Four* is . . . ."

12. How finished is the film? What else needs to be done to it?

13. Marvel's Avi Arad claims that he "burned" the film, although it survives in bootleg versions. Do you think there is a print, negative, or other high-quality copy hidden or forgotten somewhere? Do you think it will ever be released? What would it take to release it? Is there profit potential?

14. The Fantastic Four films have not been as successful as some of Marvel's other movies. What is the difficulty with successfully transferring the Fantastic Four from the page to the screen?

15. There is a legend circulating that your father is hairstylist Vidal Sassoon known for his hair salons and hair products. Is this true? Other than the similarity in surnames, how do you think this story got started?

*

Most questions I could recycle in other interviews regarding the film. The last question is specific to the director. I deliberately placed that question last for several reasons. First, it is not relevant to the story of *The Fantastic Four* and I had no idea if Oley Sassone would be the kind of person that I could ask this question of. On the one hand, it's potentially funny and interesting. On the other hand, it's potentially insulting and/or too personal. For all I knew, they were related and there had been a traumatic split in the relationship and my question would unnecessarily reopen an old and deep wound. As we made our way through the interview, Sassone felt like the sort who would not be insulted by the question, so I asked it, got a good story out of it, and everything was fine. I did preface the question at the start with something along the lines of "I don't know if this is a sensitive area or not so if you don't want to get into this, that's perfectly fine" to indicate that I knew I could be treading on potentially difficult ground and to give Sassone (and myself) an easy out. It's okay to ask direct questions. It's okay to ask tough questions. Sometimes you can phrase difficult questions delicately; other times you can't. The questions should never seem like an attack. Little else shuts down conversation—or starts an argument—so quickly as an attack, perceived or real. If there is a Tao of interviewing it might be the following: Push without bulldozing. Press but stop short of piercing. Be firm but not inflexible. Listen while you speak, but do not speak while you listen. Have an open plan. Keep a goal in mind when being spontaneous. The best interviews are not interviews. The best interviews are conversations.

Looking back at the list of questions for Sassone, you'll notice that almost all of those question can be reused. Since this appears to violate some of my earlier commandments about question-making, let's discuss the design of that first list. Originally, this interview was going to be part of a different book of interviews about Roger Corman and New World Pictures for which I was conducting interviews and serving as an associate editor. *The Fantastic Four* came a few years after the New World Pictures era, so the idea was that I would individually interview a few people from the film and then compile that into a roundtable interview that would form an appendix at the back of the book. Thus, I intended that first list to be a universal list of questions I could use to interview the directors and a couple of the film's actors. However, so many people responded positively to requests for interviews—unlike the New World Pictures project—that I quickly realized this had the potential to become its own project. Long story short, with the encouragement of Mark Sikes who made a documentary on the film, the backing of my publisher and first and foremost the knowledge and blessing of the general editor of the New World Pictures project who had brought me onto that project, I broke the Fantastic Four interviews off and made *The Fantastic Four* its own collection. However, the first few interviews, including the one with Sassone, were designed as part of that original roundtable concept in which I would use one list of questions for multiple people. A lot of those questions I kept as I interviewed other people, and some of the questions I dropped so that we could have multiple viewpoints without certain questions becoming too rote. By the time I knew *The Fantastic Four* was going to be its own project, I already had the first few interviews completed and cleared. If I had known at the start that this was going to become its own project, I would have made more of that first list of questions unique, though the interviews still found their own directions and other questions came up (as they usually do) that deviate from my original list. Also, as I progressed through the interviews, I sometimes contacted previous interviewees with new questions or edited the same questions to look a little less repetitive (both of which I will talk more about later on).

I'll give a final example of questions from further on in that project after I knew it was going to be a full project of its own. Contrary to the previous set of questions, most of these are specifically for Roger Corman.

*

1. Tell us about Bernd Eichinger's initial pitch to you to make *The Fantastic Four*.
2. When did production begin?
3. Did you ask for anything else beyond his initial offer?
4. What happened after you made the film?
5. Eichinger makes the big deal with Fox. What does that mean for the film you made?
6. Was there a strategy regarding whom to cast or how to cast? Did you have someone particular in mind?
7. What was your initial investment in the film? Did you have to invest money upfront as well?
8. Do you think Eichinger planned to release the film, or was making it just a way for him to keep the rights?
9. So how did Marvel get involved in terms of buying up the film?
10. Do you know if anyone at Marvel ever saw the film?
11. How much or how little did Eichinger have to do to retain the rights? We know he had to be in production, but was he required to have a finished film or did he just have to start production? What was the minimum he had to do?
12. Why do you think he decided to complete the whole thing?
13. Did you interact with Stan Lee?
14. Why did you pick Oley Sassone as director?
15. What did you think of the completed version of the film?
16. When did you find out the film would not be released?
17. When Marvel bought the film, did they pay you anything?

18. The director, cast, and crew were and are disappointed that the movie did not come out. What would you say to them now?

19. At the end of *How I Made a Hundred Movies in Hollywood and Never Lost a Dime* you wrote, "There are parts of me in all of my films." Are there parts of you in *The Fantastic Four*?

20. Over the years you've discussed your interest in Freudian psychology and offered Freudian readings of your films. Will you give us a Freudian reading of *The Fantastic Four*?

21. How difficult was it to show the various powers of the Fantastic Four?

22. Reed Richards, Johnny Storm, Sue Storm, Ben Grimm, and Victor Von Doom—which of the film's major characters do you most identify with?

23. What happened to the copies of the film?

24. If it had been released, how well do you think it would have done in the box office?

25. Do you think that the film will ever be released?

26. What did you think of the 2005 version?

27. Anything else you want to talk about, add, clarify, or elaborate on?

Four of the last five are not necessarily ones that only Corman could answer, but since they are more generic and I didn't know how much time we would have, I placed them last since they are not as important. As an additional note, the final question ("Anything else you want to talk about, add, clarify, or elaborate on?") is an unofficial question I usually ask as a final question in every interview as a chance to see if the interviewee has something else they want to say.

Now that we've looked at some sample lists of questions, let's delve into some other points about making interview questions. The interviewer's main toolbox consists of who, what, when, where, why, and how. Questions beginning with these words are open questions that call for the respondent to supply an answer. The answer may be specific, complex, short, or long, but the respondent supplies an answer they have to develop. Close-ended questions either call for a binary answer—usually yes/no—or ask the respondent to pick an answer from a set of possibilities you provide. Some examples are multiple choice questions or scale questions that measure how much the respondent agrees with a particular statement. Occasionally asking yes/no questions can be useful, especially for purpose of clarification. However, yes/no questions do not always develop conversations and dialogue. Multiple choice and scale questions very rarely have a place in interviews. These are used chiefly for customer surveys or testing purposes or other instances in which the responder and/or the person tabulating the responses doesn't have much time to spend.

Mirroring is a variation of the yes/no question that can encourage respondents to elaborate and provide depth on something they have just talked about. Someone supplies an answer and then you rephrase/restate it. You don't want to just parrot what they said. It won't have the same effect and it could sound like you are making sure you heard them correctly. The point is not to get them to repeat what they said but to get them to elaborate on what they said.

The following example is from an interview I conducted with Lloyd Kaufman, co-founder of Troma Entertainment, about his involvement in *The Fantastic Four*. The story was that Bernd Eichinger, who had the rights to make the film, approached Kaufman at some point about Troma making the film. Kaufman's memory was a little hazy. Close to the end of the interview as his recollections suggested a basic shape and timeline, I used mirroring to make sure that what I thought he said was accurate, to put together a basic sequence of important events, and to pull together a cohesive narrative that our talk seemed to have uncovered. I also want to be clear that without the prior context of our interview, my questions and statement might be a little more leading than what they actually were. You can see that I drew a lot of value and information from Lloyd just by saying to him what he already said to me.

*

Some people have speculated that the movie was never going to be released. It was just a way for Bernd to hold onto the rights because those rights were due to expire. Did Bernd ever give you an indication that this was not going to be a real film or that it wasn't going to be a film that would be released?

No. Not that I recall. [*laughs*] Then I definitely would have turned it down. I'm pretty sure that I let him know that we had to be involved in distributing it. By the time we got through, I think he knew what Troma's business model was. I would have had to direct it, for sure. I would have had to have some kind of control over it. I think he probably knew that might not be the best relationship. Again, I have total respect for him and his body of work. I regret . . . Especially if half a million bucks was involved. That's a lot of dough.

Did you just finally tell him Troma wasn't going to do the film or how . . .

No. I just never heard from him again.

So you had your first and maybe second conversation and he just never . . .

I think he realized . . . I can't say I turned it down. But when he first approached me, he sounded like he wanted me to do it. Then, I think my frame of mind and Troma's business model, shooting in the East, and shooting on location, and Troma having to be involved in distribution, were all factors. If we couldn't get what we wanted on that level, I certainly wasn't going to do it, and in my head it sounded like it was going to be a shitty fee, a bad experience, I would piss off Stan Lee, and I would piss off the Troma fans.

Let me see if I've got this right. What it sounds like is that you never told him no and he never told you no. After the first or second conversation, he just never called you back or followed up, but, if he had, it's very likely you would have pulled out anyway because it didn't seem like . . .

Well, I did think he asked me if I was interested in doing it. I mean he called me in because I think he thought he wanted me to do it. I don't recall him ever offering me the job, but me made it sound like he was an admirer and that he wanted me. I don't know if that's before he talked to Roger Corman or after he talked to Roger Corman. He was probably shopping like everybody does. He's a businessman.

I see what you're saying. He might have had a conversation or two with you, and then he talks to Roger Corman, works out a deal with him, and that's why he never gets back in touch with you.

That's probably it. And I probably really didn't get very interested. I really wasn't interested for the reasons I've told you. It wasn't that I called him; I don't believe I ever called him back. In fact, I'm certain I never called him back. We had a couple of meetings. We had a couple of discussions. If he wanted me, he could have called me back. I think it was pretty clear that I would be a little bit difficult and that I wouldn't fit. It wasn't a good fit.

So Bernd didn't pursue the conversation but neither did Troma.

Exactly.

*

Besides developing the actual questions, how you lay them out on the page is important. Type and print the questions out. Type them out so that you can read and share them. Print them out so that you do not have to fiddle around with opening computer screens. You may also need that open computer screen for something else such as quickly looking up information during the interview. Printing questions allows you to check them off and make notes as you go. Generally, I have a printed copy out along with an open computer screen on my laptop and an open screen on my iPad. This gives me one place to look at for questions and to make notes, and two separate locations for computer screens. The reason I keep both screens open is that sometimes we may pause the interview while I quickly look up a year, name, date, or other information we need. Other times, I may be looking something up as the interviewee is talking. I don't want them to be distracted or think I am distracted. They may hear me clacking away on the laptop keyboard, but they won't hear me typing on the iPad.

I also number the questions to make them easier to follow for me and the interviewee. Another reason I type them out is besides having a copy I can easily find later as opposed to trying to unearth the only copy of a handwritten set, is that I can send a copy to the interviewee ahead of time.

It's great to ask unique, creative questions but be careful of choosing questions that might be too quirky or that seem creative but are actually very generic. If it's a question you've heard before, then it's probably not very original. If you could have lunch with any person living or dead, who would you pick and why? If you could travel to any place in time, past or future, where would you go? What is your favorite color? These are boring questions. Don't ask them.

What's the theme or the message of (blank)? That's one of my favorite questions to ask. Some of that is probably my background interpreting, analyzing, and teaching literature. Thinking about theme answer urges us to reflect on the overall, bottom-line message of the work. Our response says as much about us as it does about the work. When I ask an interviewee about the theme of, for example, a movie, I am asking at least as much about them as I am the movie. The following exchange with Sid Haig is an example of this. A couple of sentences before the end of his previous answer, he said, "Other people had other fears and their death was connected to their fear in some way." I incorporated this idea into my next question about the theme of the film.

*

My next question was doing to be does *Galaxy of Terror* have a message, but do you think that is the message, that the things we fear ultimately can or will kill us if we give them power over us?

Absolutely. Absolutely. There's two big real killers. That's fear and guilt. [note: This gave me an idea for two follow-up questions not in my original list of questions.]

What do you fear most?

Not being able to create.

What do you think Roger Corman fears most?

Not being able to create.

*

I suppose I could have also asked him about something he felt guilty about, but based on the general feel of the interview, I'm not sure I felt comfortable doing that. Guilt, I think, is even more personal than fear; fear may concern a hypothetical event that could happen to us, but guilt usually originates from something we have done (or failed to do) and carries a sense of responsibility, regret, and possible shame. Figuring out how far you can push is something you have to play by ear and can only decide during the course of the interview. For this reason, I would place possibly controversial questions towards the end such as this one with Barry Schrader who created the soundtrack for *Galaxy of Terror*.

*

The booklet included with *Galaxy of Terror* states that it has been listed in the top 50 worst movies of all time. Is this fair?

Anyone can make a list. Who made that list? You could make all kinds of lists if you wanted to. I'm sure that a lot people think that it's an absolutely horrible piece of junk, but it does have a cult following.

*

Another technique I use is to take an activity the interviewee engages in and ask them to compare it to the topic I am interviewing them about. Here is an example with Martin Kove:

I read that you have a black belt in karate and continue to train in martial arts. What lessons or principles can you apply from karate to filmmaking, Roger Corman, acting, and/or Hollywood?

Discipline.

Sheer discipline.

Karate is about discipline. Karate is about focus. Karate, according to Mr. Miyagi, was defined as a defensive art. John Kreese defines it as an offensive sport. There are some people that if they win in the tournament, it's enough. John Kreese's concept is it's not about just the tournament; it's about making sure that your enemy, your opponent, doesn't get up because on the street if you let someone get up, you endanger your life. He applies the same thing from the streets to a tournament.

But in either case, acting or directing for Roger Corman or anyone, it's discipline. It's discipline to do your homework. It's discipline to do your backstories. Discipline to really have a couple of alternatives as an actor to play with. If something doesn't work out, you have a plan B, plan C.

*

Grace Zabriskie's character from *Galaxy of Terror* had some unique lines, so I asked her what some of these mean:

There are certainly some memorable lines. Can you tell us what these three lines mean? "An oxer in a breather bar," "Fame is the food that dead men eat," and "The master sends meat, but the devil sends cooks."

I don't remember asking what those lines meant. I remember knowing that I had to decide what they meant. So: "An oxer in a breather bar"—that was easy. I decided it was related to the fact that there are now bars where you go in and take oxygen. *Oxer* refers to someone who is into oxygen. "Fame is the food that dead men eat" is a way of saying that lasting fame really comes only after death. "The master sends meat, but the devil sends cooks" means we can thank God for our food, but the devil sure can fuck it up.

As we learn, the Planet Master *is* God, in a sense. The quote presupposes a culture in which the Planet Master is indeed God in terms of what their concept of God is. That's a huge thing to understand.

*

Besides the depth of her response, what's great about her answer is that she connects her answer to a larger idea about the movie.

Sometimes even relatively flat or basic questions can elicit memorable responses. I have begun interviews by asking for basic background information about a respondent. Here is an example from Zabriskie that gave me more than I expected:

*

Let's begin with some background about yourself. How did you get started working in movies and television?

(pauses) Dear God in heaven, I just can't get interested in that question.

*

I love that answer. It's the first question I asked and I quickly learned a lot about her because her answer establishes from the beginning that she is going to call it as she sees it. First questions are important because they also send a first impression. While you may have already communicated with your interviewee, the first question of the interview still sets the tone for the actual interview. If you have arranged the interview through a manager or media person, then the first question is the first contact you will have with the interviewee. It's a little like chess; do you go for a bold opening move or play it safe? I'd advise against going all-out on the opening question. If you start with a tamer or more general question, you can build rapport and work towards a deeper or more controversial question later. We'll look at this more in later sections, but you can reorder the questions after the interview and move a more interesting question and answer to an earlier position in the interview draft and/or eliminate a question and answer that lacks strength and impact.

Although I made an earlier analogy between preparing questions and having a script ready, remember that you are not as locked in to your questions as what the comparison implies. I have conducted interviews in which I went through all of the questions, and that worked fine. In other situations, treating the question list as an inviolable checklist dictating that I must complete each and every question in order as I typed it would have stunted the interview. You can reorder questions, skip questions, change questions, and/or add questions during the interview. It's okay to make adjustments, to modify and improvise. However, you can't deviate from a plan unless you have a plan. Don't try to wing it unless absolutely necessary (as I'll talk about later with Pete Von Sholly). That *can* work. However, it is good to have some sense or idea of what you want to ask. Better to have more questions than you need than to need more questions than you have.

How Many Questions Do You Need?

In terms of how many questions to make, I would say at least ten to twelve. You shouldn't need more than twenty-four. I had seventeen questions prepared for Sid Haig, and we didn't even talk for twenty minutes, even with the on-the-fly questions I introduced. He was very to the point. I've had other situations in which the interviewee needed very, very little prompting to talk and I could probably have come to the interview with just five questions and been totally fine. I wouldn't count on that, and, as with most things, it's better to come in over-prepared. It's easier to make in-the-moment decisions about cutting questions than it is to create new questions in the midst of the interview. If you veer on the side of caution and make lots of questions, be sure that you still cover your core questions. You can always try to have it both ways by preparing, say, two dozen questions and moving eight to twelve of them further down the page in an "if we have time" section consisting of questions you would like to ask if there is time but that can be skipped if there is not time.

If you don't use all of the questions you create, great. That means you had plenty of material. What is unused might find a place in a later interview.

Sending Reminders with Questions Ahead of Time

If possible, it's a courteous gesture to send a reminder with questions the day before. Sending questions ahead of time allows the interviewee to think some on them. You may get answers that are more thorough. If you are interviewing someone about a topic not from the recent past, they have a chance to review that earlier material. Sending questions ahead of time also allows the interviewee time to think about or review items they may have forgotten about. For example, more than one person I talked to for the New World Pictures project told me that they had not seen a particular film they had worked on for some time and wanted to a chance to review it or a particular scene before we talked. Also, when people know what's going to happen, they generally feel better about being a part of it. Sending a reminder with questions is a final chance to make sure that everyone is on the same literal and figurative page. If you are unsure, you can always ask your contact if they want you to share questions ahead of time or not. The offer to do so—even if refused—sends a message that you are professional, prepared, and taking the interview opportunity seriously.

About Voice Recorders and a Horror Story About Malfunctions AKA "The Prince Method"

Originally, I bought a pair of inexpensive recorders that had a lot of high customer ratings. I didn't really know then what I wanted or needed in a quality recorder and I thought I would only be conducting a couple of interviews, which meant that it didn't really matter what I used because I wouldn't be using it very much. Looking back, I think these high ratings were mostly a reflection of the price (the one upside is buying something very cheap gives you a way to figure out what features you want with minimal investment). Rather than tell you everything that was wrong with that model now, I'll tell you what you should look for in a quality recorder that you will likely use again and again. Look to spend between $50 and $100 on a good piece of equipment; once you approach $200, you will probably find diminishing returns. I use a Sony ICD UX-560. As of this writing, the current version of that model is the ICD UX-570. I picked the model I use because I have had good experience with Sony products in the past. I have found them easy to use, long-lasting, and they have the features I need. You want something that is easy to use with menus and functions that are clear and organized and buttons that are large enough and spaced far enough apart that you don't have to worry about accidentally activating the wrong function. A headphone jack is essential because it will make it easier to hear the playback. The ability to start and stop easily during the transcription is an absolute must. Of course, you want a recorder that gives you good sound. By good sound, I do not mean something you can make bootleg live recordings with. "Good sound" means you can hear the other party clearly and distinctly. My recorders have a lot of features I rarely use such as the option to set the playback speed. Being able to slow down the recording is occasionally useful in order to hear a word—usually a name or place—that sounds unclear. Although I cannot type fast enough to keep up with the recording at regular speed, I find that slowing the recording down to a pace I can keep up with doesn't really make the process any easier or faster. For you it might. Or perhaps you can type so quickly, that *speeding* up the playback speed is an advantage. You'll have to decide what options you need.

Whatever you get, remember that reliable equipment saves you time and mental energy.

Let me tell you about the horrible event that pushed me to upgrade my equipment. I interviewed Durinda Wood early in the Corman project and learned this lesson through experience, which is often the best teacher but exacts the highest price. I used the two cheap recorders I mentioned earlier. We finished the interview and anxious to begin the first pass at transcribing the interview, I sat down, turned on the recorder, and discovered to my horror that it simply was not there. There was no trace of it. I turned on the second recorder and nothing was there either. To this day, I am not sure what happened. I turned both recorders on. I know they were both running. It seems bizarre they both behaved in the exact same way—they captured nothing at all—on the same interview, but it is possible. Other than operator error, I don't have a better explanation than simultaneous catastrophic failure, but it seems equally strange—though possible—that I made the same egregious mistake with both recorders on the same session.

Either way, here's the point: Don't use cheap tools. Even if the interview had not evaporated from both recorders, the equipment was difficult to use. The buttons were small. The fast forward function was very slow. The sound was fuzzy and muffled. Maddeningly, I found that when I paused too long during the transcription process, the recorder forgot where I was and I had to fast forward from the beginning of the interview to wherever I had left off. The two best things I can say about them are 1) they taught me firsthand what I really needed in a recording device and 2) I no longer have those pieces of junk.

Ultimately, I was able to salvage the situation. However, I did not offer every detail about the situation.

*

Hello Durinda:

I have a draft of the interview attached. I reviewed the tape last night and discovered my equipment was picking up something on my end that made it very hard for me to hear large portions of the tape. Realizing I would be working largely from notes and memory,

I went ahead and put down everything I could recall while it was freshest in my mind. I think I captured most of it, but there is also a lot that probably didn't make it in. So feel free to add in anything you want including any ideas, points, or memories that have surfaced after we talked. If I left something out, it was not deliberate; for some things I captured the larger point but not all of the details. And if there are any factual errors, please correct those or let me know.

I think I stayed true to the spirit of your words and of the interview even if I was not able to work as directly with the recording as I usually do. Please feel free to change anything you like. And please don't let me put words in your mouth unless you are happy with those words. I will say that I think we both sound pretty good here. When you have made whatever edits and additions you want, I'll take a look at it, proofread again, and see if I have any further thoughts. Again, thanks so much for the interview. It was a real pleasure.

Best,
William

*

Of course, most of this was true. I did appreciate the interview. I did discover the interview was lost the same day that we conducted it. I did sit down and try to put down on the page everything I could recall. I did have a major technical malfunction. I just omitted the important fact that I had absolutely no recorded trace of our actual interview and, therefore, not a single word of the typed interview came from it. Why wasn't I completely forthcoming about what had happened? To be clear, nothing about Wood seemed tough or unforgiving, but I think I was scared that I would sound totally incompetent and the response from the other end might be something along the lines of "Too bad for you. You had your chance and wasted my time." I suppose that still could have been the response to the version of events I gave, but at least what I said didn't make it sound like the interview experience had been a total waste of her time. It's always possible that although she didn't know for sure what had happened on my end, she found my explanation suspect but decided for whatever reason to go along with my story anyway. It's Hollywood, so I hardly doubt I am the first person to round the edges of the truth.

Wood generously offered to do some content editing of the interview. Most of it was in the form of additions and deletions of material as opposed to rephrasing or rewording content. Oddly, there were parts I am sure she had originally said that she later deleted and explained it was because it did not sound like her and there were other parts I know I took greater liberties with in terms of content and phrasing that she left untouched. Of course, memory is unreliable and I was hardly in a position to put up any resistance to any changes she made. Ultimately, the interview came out several hundred words longer than the original one I developed and went through a total of three drafts. There were a few points the final draft leaves out that I think would have made it a better interview, but that assessment is not unique to this interview, and I'm just glad I came out of this episode with a strong, finished interview. Of the three drafts, the final is the strongest. I attribute that to the extra attention, time, and thought Wood gave it. Focusing on the interview drafts probably dredged up some additional thoughts and memories and helped clarify what was already there. Still, it's not a method I ever care to use again.

I felt a little better when I remembered that Prince had a stretch in the 1990s when he refused to allow interviewers to use a tape recorder or make any notes. In a 1998 interview with *Guitar World*, he explained that "To me, a tape recorder is like having a contract . . . When there is no tape recorder, our relationship is based on trust." If I had interviewed Prince under those stipulations, I have a feeling that if we did a second interview, Prince would have handed me a recorder and said, "I read the first interview. Please, use this for our second."

What Should You Have Ready Right Before the Interview?

You want to choose as quiet of a space with as little traffic in and out as possible. Most of us will not have a Batcave to retire to and a personal assistant to hold calls and keep people at bay. Generally, I conduct my interviews from the kitchen table in my house. My wife stays quiet and we don't have any small children. Our dogs have been good about not barking, but I have heard their tip-tapping around in the background on our bare floors a few times on the recorder during playbacks. I assume the parties on the other end either don't notice it, don't pay it much mind, or have been patient with the occasional, sometimes unavoidable "sounds of life." However, I would not suggest pushing that patience too much. No audio devices should be playing at any level, no one should be talking, and the general environment should be as still and quiet as possible. I set up at the kitchen table because, due to the configuration of my house, it's the best place to respond from if someone knocks on the door or the dogs need something. Also, the kitchen table gives me the most elevated and open space to set up and spread out everything I need.

I place a typed set of questions on the table. I have my laptop open and my iPad available also in case I need to pull a file up from my computer or research anything. I have something to write with available. I have something to drink that I keep away from papers and electronics. I also use the speaker for the cellphone and place it on the table. I use two (2) voice recorders, and I place each of them about six inches on either side of my phone.

What Time Do You Call?

Sometimes the interviewee or their media person, secretary, or assistant will contact you. Sometimes it's the other way around. Either way, be ready. If you will be the one to call, try to call as on the dot as possible. Calling before time can look impatient and your interviewee may have been counting on those extra few minutes to get prepared for your interview or finish a task. Calling after the scheduled time looks unprofessional and opens up the possibility that you may have forgotten about the interview. Also, waiting makes people anxious.

Silence/Pausing After Questions and Answers

Often, silence makes us uncomfortable. We are forced to sit with ourselves. We aren't sure what the other party thinks or feels. We wonder if something is wrong. We aren't used to not having some sort of nonstop noise or chatter to fill up the space and distract us. We lack patience. For whatever reason, we rush to fill what feels like emptiness. Don't be too quick to move to the next question. Interviewees may be recollecting or thinking about what to say. After that pause, good content may come forth. If you are going question-by-question, the interviewee has given a thorough answer, and there is a lengthy pause or you can tell by the content and/or tone that they are at the end of their answer, then move on. Sometimes after you ask the first few questions, you can tell how long the interviewee is going to answer, you can sense a change in tone when they are at the end, and if they are not pausing except at the ends of questions, then you can feel when it is time to ask the next question. Don't worry too much about trying to speed through and get to every question; there's no absolute checklist you must complete or quota you have to fulfill. You can always reorder your questions in the moment and move something more important up in the queue if you sense or know you are running out of time and won't be able to get to everything. You can't make a tree grow by pulling on it. Let the interview find its own pace. Listen. Breathe.

What Does "Off the Record" Mean?

Well, it means pretty much what it sounds like it means: Don't repeat or transmit whatever the information is that the interviewee has asked to remain private, unpublished, uncirculated, and off the record. Sometimes people want to spill a little juice on an associate or situation. People gossip and repeat rumors. They want to share a hunch, theory, or hypothesis. Perhaps they want to vent. I've had people tell a story or share an impression and realize afterwards that perhaps that would best be kept between us. I have also had folks share something with me that they thought would help enlarge my understanding but they didn't want to share that something or go on record as being the one that shared it. It could even be just innocuous chitchat that they don't care for the world to overhear. If you have to share the recording, then you should pause it so that whatever the interviewee says is truly off the record. If you are the only one who will have the recording, then you may not feel that is necessary. You can also go back and use an audio or video trimmer to cut out whatever doesn't belong on the record. However, that adds another step to the process and means you have to very, very sure you don't leave anything unwanted in whether it is by request (e.g., a clandestine romance on the set) or dictated by common sense (e.g., a phone number).

Originally, for the New World Pictures project we were asked to send a copy of the audio that would ultimately be directed to some sort of archive. I did that for the first interview and then declined after that for several reasons. After that first interview, interviewees gave me information that would not have been appropriate to pass along such as off-the-record anecdotes and personal contact information. I was very concerned I might pass over and leave something that should be cut out. Also, I was telling interviewees that they would have the opportunity to review the draft I would send to the general editor. Archiving the entire recording or a version that even if trimmed would not match up to the version that interviewee agreed on struck me as a possible contradiction and breach of their trust. Also, if I told them about archiving the tape, I worried that they might close up and become more guarded during the interview. Tenseness and inhibition are the opposite of the comfort and openness that are part of a good interview. However, not telling them about sending on the recording seemed unethical—and no one said, suggested, or implied that I should do that. Getting a good printed interview was a higher priority for me than generating archival material, so the solution I settled on was to hold back the tape and not pass a copy along for archiving.

At the End of the Interview

Once we reach the finish line, I always ask the interviewee if there is anything else that they want to talk about, add, or clarify. If you are not absolutely sure of the spelling of a name or some other word—usually it's a name—ask the interviewee to spell it for you. While you can ask as you go through the interview, if you do not want to break the flow of conversation, keep a running list of words as you go and ask after the interview for their correct spelling. If you are working on a larger project, this end phase is also the time to ask for a referral or if the interviewee can think of anyone else that would be good for you to talk to for your project. If they are going to review a draft, I remind them that I will send that to them and I give them some sort of general timeframe for when I will do that. If they do want to look at a draft and I do not already have an email address—perhaps all I have is a phone number because someone else arranged the interview for me—I ask for that so that I can send a draft to them. I end by thanking them. Though, I keep the recorder running during all of this, little to any of this wrap-up will make it into the released version because, while necessary, most of this information will not be interesting (obviously, I don't share, circulate, or publish anyone's personal contact information).

Keep the Recorder Running

I press record just before I dial the interviewee's phone number. I don't stop recording until after I hang up. You can always choose not to include something someone says, but you can never recapture it on tape. The only exception to this is if I know I will have to share the recording with someone else and there is content that the interviewee requested I exclude from the formal account; in that situation I would pause the tape. After the interview seems to be done, the interviewee may continue talking. Often, they may relax and lower their defenses a bit. You can get some great additional content *after* the interview. I just ask the interviewee if it is okay to include what they talked about, especially if they are not going to review a draft either by choice or the publication forbids that option. Usually, you can sense when an interview is powering down, but sometimes you will get another late burst of conversation. Even if it's just a stray remark or a single sentence, you want to have that available and recorded for possible use.

Interviewing via Video

For better or worse, video is an increasingly popular option for all types of interactions that were previously conducted in-person. Although I have only conducted an interview via video once (Keith Hamilton Cobb), I have taught class many times, delivered conference papers, chaired conference panels via Zoom and the like, and a lot of that experience carries over for interviewing through a screen. The principle for video interviewing is the same as phone interviewing: Have everything you need at hand. Learn how to use your equipment beforehand, and test your equipment ahead of time. If a device isn't working, the problem may have a quick and easy fix such as turning your speakers on, up, or off of mute, but it will take a little time and you don't want to be hunting, fumbling, distracted, trouble-shooting, and apologizing during the interview. While we expect our phone speakers to function automatically, you may have to locate and turn on your laptop's speaker, and you may also discover that it isn't very good and that you need an external microphone. As I said, I have taught classes over Zoom. If I forget to plug in the external microphone, the class quickly indicates that they either cannot hear me or cannot hear me well. While my students tend to be flexible and helpful when I have an occasional technology issue during our dozens of semester class meetings, the interview opportunity is probably going to be a one-shot opportunity with a limited timeframe; the technology part of the process, thus, needs to be flawless.

I prefer an external microphone that I can direct and position as opposed to a built-in computer microphone. Many microphones are just plug and play; you plug it into a USB port and the microphone does the rest without you having to download and install a program or worry about compatibility (I recommend plug and play). I purchased a FIFINE K669B for $30 that has served me well. I recently upgraded equipment. I have read and heard positive reports about the Blue brand, though they are more expensive ($130 for the Blue Yeti). However, I picked a RØDE NT-USB Mini ($100). Basically, the RØDE works better for my space and I only need it for speaking, which I think it does as well as or better than the Blue Yeti. While the Blue Yeti has more application settings, I don't need a device that does four things well; I need a device that does one thing great.

I reiterate the lesson I learned the hard way from buying cheap products: Invest in decent equipment that will not fail you. Whatever microphone you use, make sure it has a tripod and is self-supporting. You do not want to have to hold the microphone, lay it on its side, or construct some kind of makeshift stand because the microphone lacks a stand or sufficient stability (avoid a top-heavy mic that may fall over if bumped). You want to have your hands free, get the best sound out of your equipment you can, and appear professional.

Keep in mind that during a telephone interview, if you take a quick look at your watch or phone, no one is going to know but you. If someone else sees you doing that, you may appear impatient. If you are in-person or on Zoom, the person you are talking to will see everything you do, so hold yourself to the same expectations for both environments. You must always appear as if the interview is the only thing that matters to you. Over the phone, you can probably get away with firing off a quick yes or no response to an important text, but I would not try that in-person or over video. Also, remember that even if you are on the phone, you should be giving the interviewee your full attention. They may not, for example, be able to see you texting or checking email, but they can hear you moving around and will be able to tell in your voice whether you are distracted or focused. Thus, while you may have a little more leeway regarding your attention span with a telephone interview, any prolonged or repeated action will be noticed by your interviewee even if they cannot see it. Besides, you want to be listening so that you can make adjustments whether that means rephrasing questions, skipping questions that have already been answered or may not seem as high a priority as time runs out, thinking of follow-up questions, realizing when you need to ask for clarification, and so forth. Another idea to keep in mind with video: While you can usually record, you should still use a vocal recorder. A decent voice recorder makes it easy to find precise points in the recording. In short, it is much easier to perform transcription with a voice recorder, which is made for that task, than to transcribe from video. However, I still record the Zoom interview as another backup and reference.

If given the choice between conducting a video interview via my phone or my laptop, I choose my laptop: higher quality, larger screen, better sound, easier to find and retrieve data, and more stability. A laptop on a table is stationary and my arm/hand won't get tired or start shaking.

Interviewing via Email

I usually present the possibility of an email interview to the interviewee. Occasionally, they pick this option or even suggest it to me. A lot of the process is the same as for an in-person interview. I email the interviewee the questions, and they answer and return them. I might ask follow-up questions later. Email is a very efficient way to do an interview as it cuts out setting up times and dates, eliminates the time spent asking questions and listening to answers, and transfers the work of typing from you to the interviewee. Although, the interviewee will probably not have many editing suggestions since they create and set virtually all of the content of the interview, I still proofread and lightly edit the interview. The biggest challenge is making sure that the interview doesn't sound too stiff and artificial because while the spoken interview can read too loosely once it is put on the page, writing what would one would normally speak can, in turn, make the interview sound overly formal and unnatural. Knowing how to construct a grammatically correct sentence and knowing how to write are not the same thing; knowing how to write something that doesn't sound like it was typed on the page is yet another level of skill—"tight but loose," as people sometimes say of the best live albums.

I once had someone who sent me over 3,000 words for the first two questions, which is a good problem to have, but it required more than proofreading and light editing. By the time the interviewee turned the complete draft in, I had over 9,000 words of content. The interviewee had delayed working on the interview and now that it was cooking on the burner, they really got on a roll. At one point, they talked about waiting so that they could get other people's viewpoints. I appreciated the attempt to present a thorough story, but I was also concerned about getting other people's memories and thoughts mixed in, so I discouraged that. I had plenty of material. Also, I needed to get this interview done.

A lot of the writing didn't seem so much to follow the list of questions as to have been inspired by them. The interviewee said they had answered the questions along the way, but there were clearly some that were unanswered. I think what happened was my interviewee got very enthusiastic about the writing and it became almost an autobiography of a certain phase of their career. There was a lot of great content in there, but it required some heavy editing in places to shape an interview out of what I had (more about editing in a later section). First, I had to smooth out all of the content, which sounded a little stilted in places, so that it read like an edited interview and not a composed autobiography. Then, I had to create questions I had not originally asked in order to pace and organize the content. Now, I needed to move some material around to help answer some of the newly-created questions. Last, I trimmed the final draft down to just under 5,000 words to remove redundancies and unrelated content. It came out well, so my point is not to say email interviews are inherently problematic, but to remind you that just because the other party types their answers does not automatically mean it will not require effort, sometimes substantial effort, on your part to shape it into a suitable final form. A lot of work may still be ahead. However, email can yield great interviews.

If the interview is someone you really want to have the experience of talking with, then don't list email as an option.

Spontaneous Interviews

On occasion a gift will drop from the heavens. Such was the case when Mick Strawn put me in touch with Pete Von Sholly. Although probably best known for his work with the *A Nightmare on Elm Street* movies, Strawn was in charge of production design and miniatures for *The Fantastic Four*. Near the end of our interview, he talked about Pete Von Sholly and told me that I should talk with him. Sholly did storyboard work for *A Shawshank Redemption, The Green Mile*, some of the *Elm Street* series and *The Fantastic Four*. The next day Strawn called me up out of the blue, gave me Sholly's number, and said that Sholly was "expecting" my call. Until Strawn had started talking about him the day before, I don't think I had even heard Sholly's name, let alone knew anything about him. I *may* have glanced at his IMDB page after we got off the phone, but most of the little I knew about Sholly came from the couple of minutes at the tail end of the previous day's interview with Strawn.

What to do? Should I, could I postpone until another day or at least maybe an hour so that I could try to conduct a little research and pull a few questions together? I performed a quick series of calculations in my head. Strawn said Sholly is "expecting your call." That sounds like he is waiting for me to call and interview him right this very minute, not "here's his number, so give him a call sometime" or "he's his contact info to set up an interview down the road." I was also concerned that if I called him to try to set up something for later, then I might lose my opportunity to talk to him. Strike while the iron is hot—as the old saying goes. While he might or might not have been offended and might or might not have been surprised if I told him that I really knew next to nothing about him and was almost completely unprepared for the interview, I didn't think I should take that risk. Also, I didn't want to make Strawn potentially look bad. Without any prompting from me, he contacted Sholly and set up this interview. He was doing me a favor and by getting involved, he was also vouching for me and indicating to both me and Sholly that he thought I could pull this off Right Now. True, I could bungle this on-the-fly interview through lack of preparation, but I felt there was more to potentially lose by delaying it than by pressing ahead, albeit less prepared than I would normally like to be. Also, I had to balance this feeling against the self-realization that I place a heavier emphasis on preparation than a lot of people, and I do a heavy amount of pre-interview work; in general, I feel there is no such thing as too much preparation as long as it is not used as an excuse for procrastination.

So, I took about couple of minutes—I was already at home anyway—to get all the equipment setup, dogs situated, something to drink on the table, open up computer screens, and take a quick glance on the internet to give myself a one-minute crash course in all things Pete Von Sholly. Then, I took a deep breath, and dialed his number.

I began with the standard sort of rank, name, and serial number and asked him to explain what exactly he did for the movie, which, of course, was the storyboarding. I focused the next few questions on the storyboarding process and what he specifically did with the storyboards for *The Fantastic Four*. This is what the interview needed to focus on but I was also looking for information I might not have thought to ask about as well as other items I could build questions from to help extend the conversation. Talking about the storyboards took us through about half of the interview. Within the first few minutes, I realized that Sholly was not what I would call standoffish or reserved, but he was not going to be someone that I could just point in a direction, cut him loose to talk, and edit it into an interview later. I recognized a fellow introvert. I was going to have to draw him out a little, which compounded the challenge, since this interview was so sudden. Along the way, I learned that he had actually worked for Marvel and knew Stan Lee and Jack Kirby. Although Sholly was not as central to the film as some other people—he had little interaction with Roger Corman, for example, and was never on set—he had the deepest connection to Marvel and the co-creators of the Fantastic Four as anyone I talked with. He talked more, more quickly, and with more feeling when we talked about some of his Marvel memories than when we talked about the movie. Due to his deep background in comics, we talked about some of his childhood experiences, how he got involved with the movie, and we touched on a few other films he had worked on. We conversed right at thirty minutes, and I came out with about

3,300 words for the final version. Not bad at all for a pop-up opportunity.

While I still prefer to be and recommend being as prepared as possible, this experience built up my confidence and demonstrated that if you can't do as much prep work as you would like, you can still get a good interview from impromptu situations.

Release Forms and Other Agreements

Before discussing and transcribing, let's talk about authorization and release forms. Your experiences may vary, but I have never been asked to use a release form for a website interview. In fact, I asked two websites, and they told me that they have never used a release form. For print interviews, I have always used release forms. This release form was forwarded to me, and I used it for that project.

*

[name of press]
[address of press]
To Whom It May Concern:
[Your first and last name] has my permission to use material that I provided for a forthcoming [name of press] release with the working title [name of book]. I expect no remuneration from the publisher. I understand that my remarks will be published and sold throughout the world.

Signed,

[interviewee's name]

NAME: ___________________________________(Print)
DATE: _____________________________

*

Where the editor got this from or whether the editor created it, I don't know. So far, it's worked for me, but I am not guaranteeing it will work for you. The form is self-explanatory, but basically it asks for the name of the press, the name of the publication, your name, the name of the interviewee, and the interviewee's signature. The agreement is that the interviewee authorizes you to use this interview, understands that it will be published, and does not expect payment for the interview. It's short, specific, and clear. Anything long, unclear, or with legal language may need to be drafted and/or reviewed by an attorney. I am going to stop short of getting into the law or dispensing legal advice for obvious reasons. I will say that if you aren't completely sure and comfortable with what you are signing or agreeing to, DO NOT SIGN IT.

Some of my interviewees supplied images. I sent them a release form, substituting *images* for *material*. I also cut and pasted copies of each photo into the actual release form. In one situation, I had two small hang ups. In the first instance, one person put a copyright notice and his name on each photo. I sent the following email.

*

I see the "copyright . . ." on each photo. Can you remove that? As I said, I take care of credit and identification in the captions. I want things to look uniform and having that caption in the actual photo looks out of place. Also, the caption I will include is larger than the words you have in the photo, so it will be easier for readers to see your name attached to each one.

*

I thought that explaining why I wanted those words removed and assuring him that he would not only get credit but his name would be more visible would be a good strategy. He agreed.

The next challenge was that he told me his lawyer was looking the form over. Uh-oh. It's not that I was in trouble or was trying to swindle him, and, as I have cautioned, it you aren't sure about or have reservations with what you are agreeing to, don't agree to it, but lawyers are expensive and they can complicate situations. I wrote the following email and tried to be non-confrontational but clear.

*

Well, you can see what the lawyer says and we can go from there. I don't want to anticipate any issues but I do want to let you know that is the same form Craig Nevius, Chris Walker, and Mick Strawn signed for the images they are letting me use. It's a modification of the interview release form.

As for my end, I cannot sign anything long, complicated, or that I don't understand. I also can't afford to have an attorney look over anything, so if your attorney modifies anything and it doesn't make sense to me based on the words on the page—not what your attorney says it means because they are your advocate, not mine—then we may be stalled out.

My only option would to be send it to the publisher and if they say, "I wouldn't sign this" or "you need to have an attorney look at this" that may be the end. I simply do not have the resources to pay an attorney to look at and possibly go back and forth with paperwork. Again, I hope this is not the case but I wanted to let you know that since it seems the attorney didn't say "everything looks good. Proceed."

*

He explained that, basically, he had lent images to various publications in the past and had problems with them then selling those images without his permission. He gave me this passage to add: "I, [first and last name], give you permission to use my personal images for this book [Title here] and only this book." I thought his request was understandable in the light of his previous experiences and I didn't plan on launching a t-shirt line or selling yoga mats with his images emblazoned on them. The passage is short, free of legalese, and clear, so I felt okay about using it. I inserted it into the image release form, he signed and returned it, and that was that.

Be sure anyone supplying images actually has the rights to the image and that you know it if has been previously used or not (the same is true of interviews, but I'll talk more about that later). You can use a reverse image search to see if you find anything similar on the internet. If the image has been cropped, resized, color corrected, or other otherwise modified or edited, you may not find a match even if some version of the image has been previously used, but at least it's a start and a quick, easy, and free preliminary scan worth performing just to double-check for previous usage.

Even for print interviews, most of the people I talked with said they did not normally have to sign a release form. I was not the top person in charge of the New World Pictures project, so it wasn't my call to make, and that is how I explained it. For *The Fantastic Four* project, as it was initially going to be part of the New World Pictures project, I was already asking for release forms, so I kept the trend going. I couldn't see a downside to having a signed release form in case I needed it in the future. However, getting the completed release back introduces another step into the process. If someone wants to start debating the final interview draft and hasn't given you that form, you have obligated yourself to please them.

The best time to get the signed release back from the interviewee is as early in the process as possible. At first, I would wait until the very end to get it back. Usually this was a painless process and I would get the form in a few days or so. Other times, it was at best a protracted process and, at worst, a stress-inducing hassle that drained my attention and energy. Since I was working with each interviewee on the final version, or at least making the offer to let them look at it and make edits, I occasionally had someone who basically wanted to rewrite the whole thing. How well that works depends upon how good of a writer they are and how open they are to editing suggestions.

Once, an agent I dealt with talked down to me. The email they sent in response to the first draft was much tougher than it needed to be and from the moment we got on the phone—at their request—the anger and impatience were evident. Most of the changes they demanded were minor. I didn't have an issue making them, but the tone they were dictated to me in was very condescending and demeaning (think Miranda Priestley). Some of the complaints stemmed from misinterpretations of my questions and the intent behind them. For example, I asked a common question about influences and the representative took offense and seemed to think I was implying that their client was lazy and not putting in adequate work on each job when I meant absolutely nothing of the sort. I taped the conversation so that I had an accurate record of the changes I needed to make to attempt to please them. I just kept my cool and did my best to complete the final interview and get that release form while remaining unfazed, dedicated, and professional. If I had gotten the release upfront or not bothered with it, I wouldn't have had to endure the scorching I received. There was nothing libelous, scandalous, inflammatory, or otherwise pursuable—in my opinion—in a more formal, legal way, so once the final version came out, the agent could have sucked it up, fumed, stewed, and/or spewed venom at me and I would not have had to entertain any of it, especially since the recording completely supported that first draft I sent for review.

I will add that the agent had originally agreed to an interview and I think they represented other potential contacts, but after having had that experience, not needing any more interviews for that project, and deciding I had enough of the bad treatment and bad attitude, I did not try contact them for any further interviews with either them or anyone they represented. I don't need that in my life. However, I still expressed my thanks when it was all done and I sincerely remain grateful for their help facilitating and coordinating the interview, and, I assume, either convincing the interviewee to agree to an interview with me or supporting the interviewee's openness and willingness to do it. If nothing else, I can say that dealing with one difficult person is good practice for dealing with the next difficult person of which there seems to be no shortage of in this world. And by having worked closely with them and satisfied them in whole, I was pretty much assured I would not hear any more fussing from them after publication, so maybe I paid upfront and went ahead and got a tough situation entirely behind me.

What would happen if you sent the final version of the interview to someone, there was no agreement on the edit, they refused to sign the form, and you published the interview nonetheless? I don't know because I've never taken that path. Once I sent a release form to an interviewee, I have always gotten it back.

Generally, I just attach the release form or forms to an email. I ask the recipient to sign and email it back. Occasionally folks print it out, sign it, take a picture of the signed form, and then email or text it to me. That works, too. The only real complication I ran into during the return process was someone who for some reason tasked their son with sending the form back to me. Why this person didn't just do it themselves I have no idea. The son was put in charge and when the son didn't do it and I told the parent, the parent told me the child was supposed have sent me the form weeks ago. I was given the son's phone number and told to call him and express the parent's displeasure. Words such as *pissed* and *bullshit* were used by the parent. Yikes. I wasn't sure how seriously to take the request/order to ream the son, and I didn't know whose fault—parent or child—it was, but I was just wanted the form back and was not interested in stepping into any family conflict or reprimanding anyone. Eventually, the parent emailed it back to me themselves. About a month later, I emailed the interviewee about another potential project. Without responding to me, they forwarded the email to a representative with whom I had a couple of conversations and then the idea just faded away. The interviewee and I never had direct communication about it and they didn't completely shoot it down because they forwarded my email to a representative instead of just ignoring it, but I feel like if they had really wanted to pursue the idea, then they would have. Ideas don't manifest into completed projects for all sorts of reasons, but the difficulties with the release form process may have left a bad taste in their mouth and created residual feelings of tension or frustration that could have been the difference maker. I'll probably never know, but I'm sure it didn't help.

A few more ideas to keep in mind. Always thank people for giving you back the release and always thank them again for the interview. Though digital methods are becoming more and more the standard, I have read of presses that want a physical form with the original signature mailed to them. Check with your particular press or publishing venue and give them at least the minimum that they request. I have never had an interviewee consent to an interview, finish the interview, and then refuse to sign a release form, but refusal can happen. Although it was not one of my interviewees, one of the associate editors for the New World Pictures project had a subject complete all steps of the interview process except for the release form, and then they refused to return the form because the book was for profit. Two years later, I encouraged him to take a final shot at getting it but advised him not to get his hopes up. Our reasoning was all of the work had been done, one more email would not take much effort, and the potential reward (the entire interview) was big. The analogy I used was the lottery: It doesn't take much to enter and there's a huge payoff, but don't count on winning. He tried one more time and, to my surprise, his interviewee finally consented and returned the release. We don't have a clue as to why.

One compromise between no agreement and a physical release form is an oral agreement. I have never actually used this, but if I were to I would probably try something like the following: "Please state your first and last name. [wait for them to state their first and last name.] Do you consent for this interview to published in print and/or online, understand that it may be edited, and that you will *not* be compensated for it?" My guess is that would not be as good as a signed release form, but it is better than nothing at all. If I were to use this, I would put it at the start of the interview for several reasons. It will be easy to find on the recording and you will not have to fast forward to the end. Also, if there is some misunderstanding on the part of the interviewee, better to find this out at the beginning of the interview than at the end. The potential disadvantage to starting the interview this way is that it immediately injects a feeling of formalness and seriousness that may put the interviewee on guard. I've heard it said than any contract or agreement—oral, typed, handshake—is only as good as the parties on each end of it. A contract is like insurance. You may not be required to carry it and you probably won't need it very often or at all, but when you do, you will be very glad you have it and you will never wish you had picked less coverage.

As you are probably starting to realize, release forms can be a chore without clear reward, but they can be useful in a dispute should one ever arise. Whether their anticipated usefulness is worth more or less than the added labor it takes to get them, is a decision you have to make. Whether you get a release form or not—especially if you don't get one—save all correspondence, recordings, and any other material relating to the interview as backup so that you have additional documentation. I will add that with most interviewees—not all—getting the release form was an easy process and that even when it was not, the feelings of struggle I felt at the time fade more and more as time goes by.

As a final thought on release forms, you will notice that although I have summarized parts of certain email correspondence, the only person I have directly quoted is myself. While I doubt there would be an issue, I err on the safe side and just don't feel comfortable directly publishing emails. It may or may not be illegal, but it feels uncomfortable in this situation. While the content may not seem like a big deal and there is nothing included in any of the emails saying that I cannot reproduce them—whether that is even or always enforceable or not, I am unsure—I don't need to quote them word-for-word, so why run a risk?

Stay Organized

Earlier, we talked about organization and how to make a simple spreadsheet that is also easy to use, read, and update. Let's talk about organizing individual files. I suggest making a folder in your computer. If this is an individual interview, I would make a folder titled with the interviewee's first and last name. If this is an individual interview but it is for a publication you regularly write for, you can place your interview file within that folder. This assumes you have an individual folder for multiple writings for a single publication, so you should have such folders set up and titled according to the name of the publication. For big projects such as a compilation of interviews, title the folder according to the book or subject. For example, I titled the folder for the series of interviews I completed for the New World Pictures / Roger Corman project "Corman." For the *Forsaken* project about Corman's unreleased *The Fantastic Four*, I named the folder "Fantastic Four." Given that I have written other papers and developed presentations on the Fantastic Four (the movie series, the comic, and the characters), titling the folder "Forsaken" would probably have been a better move, but I didn't have the book title then and the writing I have done about the Fantastic Four besides *Forsaken* has been after *Forsaken*. Of course, you can always retitle folders. Really, you just need something clear, related, and that you can easily find, especially if you take an extended break from the project for some reason. For this current project, I titled the folder "BM Interview Book." So far, I have the working, in-process draft of the book and a few files that are copies of emails because they contain some good ideas that I included in the initial pitch. I can draw from these emails and use them as notes and topic ideas. I also have the manuscript contract and the style guide from the press. Keeping everything related to the book in one folder keeps me organized and saves me time since I don't have to dig around in my computer and email to keep pulling up relevant files that I need. Sometimes you can spend five minutes rooting around for a file, but the information in the file only takes you five seconds to find. The larger the project and the more files you have, the more you will benefit from staying organized. Just like the spreadsheet we discussed earlier, the sooner you set up your system, the easier it will be for you.

Pinning files can be helpful. The main file for this book is a pinned document. If I have, say, a music review, conference paper, or other mid-sized to small projects I am working on every or most days of the week, I pin those, too. If you have more than a handful of pinned files, pinning loses its purposes. One large project, a mid-size project, and a smaller project or a larger project and two-smaller projects should be the maximum at any given time. Everything cannot have the same level of high priority; think of senders who always attach the red exclamation mark to their emails, car alarms that go off every time the owner gets in or out of the car, and people that always talk in a loud voice. Emphasis loses its importance from overuse. If something always stands out, then it never stands out. It burns out.

Be consistent with how you title files. I've gone through various methods, and this is what I have settled on. The first three words I use in the file's title are the interviewee's first name, last name, and the word *interview*. For my initial pass, I use the word *first*. We'll talk more about transcribing and editing, but that "first" draft is the most comprehensive one in which I act more as a stenographer just getting down what was actually said as opposed to shaping, editing, and so forth. When I get what is the final draft, the one I will either send to the publication or use for the assembly of an entire book, I type the word *FINAL* in all caps, the person's first and last name, and the word *interview*. I think it's important that each draft receives its own differentiation and file. You may need or want to see your steps and reverse-engineer your editing, revision, and writing process.

A sequence of interview titles might look something like this (remember this will be alphabetized and not in chronological order of the process, though in this particular instance the chronological order matches the alphabetization):

Barry Schrader interview first draft
Barry Schrader interview second draft
FINAL Barry Schrader interview

For the interview questions, I type the person's first and last name and the words *questions*. For the interview release, I type *interview release* and the person's first and last name. This keeps all of my release forms organized. For signed releases, I type *signed release* and the person's first and last name. Again, this keeps all of the signed releases categorized and organized. I tend to use the word *interview* in most of the files because I could, for example, write or have written something else about the person that is not an interview.

If we add those files to the ones above, we have the following (again, remember this will be alphabetized):

Barry Schrader interview first draft
Barry Schrader interview second draft
Barry Schrader questions
FINAL Barry Schrader interview
Interview release Barry Schrader
Signed release Barry Schrader

As we will discuss, you might allow the interviewee the opportunity to read and comment on the interview before it officially appears. I also label those drafts as well. Assuming Schrader didn't just briefly mention a small change in the body of an email, I would take whatever files he sent and save that in a way that indicates what draft he is commenting on and that he is commenting on it. If I sent him "Barry Schrader interview first draft" and he sent back the interview with comments, edits, suggestions, remarks, or anything else that would constitute revision, I would title that as "Barry Schrader interview first draft Schrader revisions." If he didn't make comments in the interview file but sent comments for me to follow, I would make a separate file and title that "Barry Schrader revisions one" (I add *one* because we might go through this cycle again for some reason, which has happened, and I demonstrate that in the example below). When I incorporate and make those changes, that version would then become "Barry Schrader interview second draft."

A complete cycle with all the interview materials from beginning to end might look like this:

Barry Schrader interview first draft
Barry Schrader interview first draft Schrader revisions **or**
    Barry Schrader revisions one
Barry Schrader interview second draft
Barry Schrader interview second draft Schrader revisions **or**
    Barry Schrader revisions two
Barry Schrader interview third draft (if needed)
Barry Schrader questions
FINAL Barry Schrader interview

interview release Barry Schrader
Signed release Barry Schrader

Yes, it is possible that "Barry Schrader interview second draft Schrader revision" might be identical to "FINAL Barry Schrader interview" if I look at his revised second draft and don't make any changes. You might be thinking, "Well, if Schrader looks at the second draft and doesn't have comments or if I felt comfortable enough following his revisions that I didn't feel a need to send another draft to him, that means the second draft and the final draft are the same, so I don't need to make two files." Still, I think it is worth saving the same file under a second name marked *final* for the sake of organization and location (I think it is overly redundant to make a file named "Barry Schrader third draft" if there is no difference between "Barry Schrader interview second draft Schrader revisions" and "FINAL Barry Schrader interview")

However, you may have your own systems or modifications of my labeling suggestions that work best for you. I can't say there is much difference between using "Signed release Barry Schrader" and "Signed *interview* release Barry Schrader" except that the former is what I arbitrarily settled into—just apply your methods consistently. Your method doesn't have to work for anyone else, except the publisher. This isn't math class; nobody is probably going to ask to see the evidence of your process. If it works for you, then it works.

Distinguishing Between Speakers in the Print/Online Interview

The interview must make it clear to readers who is speaking and when. Unless someone tells me how they want me to do it, or I can follow an example from another interview on, for example, the same website my piece will appear on, I use two methods. For the Corman project, we use speaker tags with the interviewer's full name in bold for the first usage, the interviewee's name in bold for the first usage, and then initials for each subsequent appearance. For Robert Powell's interview with Joe Viola the identification tags look like this:

Robert Powell:
Joe Viola:
RP:
JV:

In *Forsaken,* I bold the text when I speak and I don't do anything to it when the interviewee speaks. In the following exchange with Michael Bailey Smith, the first speaker is me and the second speaker is him.

*

I really appreciate the honesty of that answer and you sharing your personal ordeal.
I'm giving you a lot more than you asked for. I'm sitting here talking about this and I have tears running down my face.

*

The advantage to the second method is that is you can always tell who is speaking. However, I've never had an interview with more than one interviewee at the time, so if I did, I would have to find a way to differentiate among speakers. By using speaker tags, an interview could have a hundred people. The disadvantage is they are visually distracting since they appear every time the interview switches speakers. Once they are condensed into initials, they are less intrusive, but contain less information. If you have a similarity in initials, the reader may be distracted. If Robert Powell (RP) interviews Randy Savage (RS) or Robert Powell (RP) interviews Rick Pepperoni (RP), the distinction between speakers becomes either confusing or nonexistent. I tend to prefer the first method of bolding the interviewer, though the use of italics is another good option. If I had it to do over again, I would make one change to the method I use in *Forsaken*. I would identify each speaker by first and last name they first time they speak, so that it is completely clear from the very start who speaks. Then, I would abandon the speaker tags after the first time. In almost all of the *Forsaken* interviews I speak first and the few times I don't the reader will quickly figure it out, but I like to be as clear as possible. In this book, I use different styles so you can get a sense of them.

Types of Transcription

There are three types of transcription: verbatim, intelligent, and edited. Verbatim is a word-for-word transcription that includes, well, every word. Speech fillers, words and phrases such as *uh, um, like*, and *you know* are included. Pauses are represented by an ellipsis (. . .). Instances of laughter or other indications of tone or emotion may be included. False starts in which the speaker starts to say something and then begins again or cuts themselves off and says something entirely different or otherwise self-corrects are included. Repetitive sentences that either say the same thing word-for-word or reword the content are included. Very, very little is left out (even coughing and background noises might be included). These are the sorts of transcriptions used in court and for police interrogations in which every little thing and the way it is said can potentially matter. While a verbatim transcription most closely resembles and reproduces how a person actually talks, they are not always enjoyable to read and often the interviewer and interviewee do not sound good. If you have ever transcribed an interview verbatim, you quickly realize that plenty of things we do and say when we talk to one another in conversation that sound perfectly natural to the ear and in the moment do not look so good when we read them on the actual page. You want the interview to sound true to the way the interviewee expresses themselves, but you also want it to sound good—natural, but readable. For example, the first content heading of the main part of the book is "Whom Do You Talk to?" Most people would probably ask "Who Do You Talk to?" I almost left it that way for that reason. If I really wanted to be proper, I would have titled it "To Whom Do You Talk?" but I thought that sounded too stiff and formal, so I split the difference. *With* sounds better than *to* and is more accurate, but if I titled the very first section "With Whom Do You Talk?" I get an image of people sitting in hard, straight-back chairs in crisp suits painfully and awkwardly trying to make conversation and feigning smiles. That also conjures an image of people closing the book because the title sounds so stiff and unnatural. That's the same reason I titled the book *Can I Quote You on That?* instead of *May I Quote You on That? Can* implies ability as opposed to *may*, which asks for permission and is closer to the actual meaning of the question. However, *May I Quote You on That?* connotes a formalness that might be off-putting to potential readers.

Here is an example of verbatim—I went back to the original recording—from the beginning of an interview I conducted with Ivan Kander.

*

Alright. Question one: According to the credits of Von Doom, you wrote, directed, edited, produced, and were responsible for the visual effects. Can we add anything else to that list that you did?

Um . . . [laughs] I mean, uh . . . I, I, I edited the film, too. Um . . . I mean with like, any time you do like an indie film project, uh, you just kind of have to wear a lot of hats. So like that's why you often see one person's name in the credits so much. So it's less about, like, this kind of weird need to do everything and more being, like, the only person that's gonna actually step up to do it. Uh . . . so that's kinda the way it was with that project. And, I mean I had tons of amazing help to put that film together, but just to get it going and, you know, a small little thing like that, you just kinda have to . . . It's a necessary evil to wear all those hats, basically [laughs].

*

Intelligent verbatim eliminates speech fillers, repetition, and pauses. Mistakes in grammar are corrected and syntax may be smoothed out. Off-topic content is eliminated. We might think of an intelligent verbatim interview as filtered and lightly edited. An edited transcription is fully edited. Sometimes the light editing of intelligent verbatim is enough. Other times, you have to dig in there and take a heavier hand and, for example, reword or restructure sentences. Remember that you do not just want to produce an interview (verbatim) or a good interview (intelligent) but the best interview and that may require medium to heavy editing (edited).

When I put together the very first draft of the interview, I create something halfway between a verbatim and an intelligent interview because I already have a sense of how to phrase the material and what not to include. At first, you may find yourself working as more of a stenographer and capturing everything exactly as it is said. There is nothing wrong with that, especially if you are new to the process. I still tend to use a kitchen sink approach and include pauses, repetitive sentences and content, sentences that trail off, self-corrections, laughter, and so on. I have found it's easier to get it all down and cut later, then to skip over something, wish I had included it, and then try to hunt around for it on the tape. I do not include filler words and phrases or background noises such as a car passing by or the speaker clearing their throat because I know I am not going to include any of that in the final draft, so there is no need to spend the time and take the energy to include it in the preliminary/original/first draft. The only thing I tend to include other than the words of the interview is laughter.

I will use the strikethrough line to indicate passages and words I cut. Insertions are in bolded brackets. Explanatory notes are bolded in brackets and begin with "note" and a colon. An intelligent verbatim draft might look like this and this would probably be my true first draft.

*

~~Alright. Question one:~~ *According to the credits of Von Doom, you wrote, directed, edited, produced, and were responsible for the visual effects.* **[(all on a budget of $11,292.83 along with some donations of time, skills, and equipment)] [note: This was in my original question but since it is for the reader's information, I cut it when I was talking with Kander.]** *Can we add anything **[else you did]** to that list* ~~that you did~~?

I edited the film, too. Anytime you **[direct]** ~~do like~~ an indie film project, you ~~just kind of~~ have to wear a lot of hats. That's **[often]** why you ~~often~~ see one person's name in the credits so much. It's less about this weird need to do everything and more being the only person that's ~~gonna~~ **[going to]** actually step up to do it. ~~that's kinda the way it was with that project. And, I mean~~ I had tons of amazing help to put that film together, but just to get it going ~~and a small little thing like that,~~ you ~~just kinda~~ have to ~~.... It's a necessary evil to~~ wear all **[of]** those hats, ~~basically~~.

*

I eliminated all of the speech fillers. In this first draft, I don't even include them because I know there is no reason to put them in the final draft. I cut out the two places where Kander laughs because they are indications more of nervous laughter than actual humor.

A fully edited draft is next. With speech fillers eliminated, now I am looking to cut out repetition, get rid of false starts, eliminate filler that don't add anything to the interview, and smooth out the general phrasing and readability of the interview.

*

Alright. Question one: According to the credits of Von Doom, you wrote, directed, edited, produced, and were responsible for the visual effects **[(all on a budget of $11,292.83 along with some donations of time, skills, and equipment)] [note: This was in my original question but since it is for the reader's information, I cut it when I was talking with Kander.]** *Can we add anything* **[else you did]** *to that list that you did?*

I edited the film, too. Anytime you **[direct]** do like an indie film project, you just kind of have to wear a lot of hats. That's **[often]** why you often see one person's name in the credits so much. It's less about this weird need to do everything and more being the only person that's gonna **[going to]** actually step up to do it. that's kinda the way it was with that project. And, I mean I had tons of amazing help to put that film together, but just to get it going and a small little thing like that, you just kinda have to . . . It's a necessary evil to wear all **[of]** those hats, basically.

*

Here's the final cleaned up and edited version of that segment of Kander's interview.

*

According to the credits, you wrote, directed, edited, produced, and were responsible for the visual effects of Von Doom (all on a budget of $11,292.83 along with some donations of time, skills, and equipment). Can we add anything else you did to that list?

I edited the film, too. Anytime you direct an indie film project, you have to wear a lot of hats. That's often why you see one person's name in the credits so much. It's less about this weird need to do everything and more about being the only person to step that's going to actually do it. I had tons of amazing help to put that film together, but just to get it going you have to wear all of those hats.

A Note About Laughter

If anyone laughs, I place the word *laughter* or *laughs* in brackets. Often, you will see interviews place [laughter] or [laughs]—sometimes italicized, sometimes not, but be consistent within the interview or collection—after the period of the sentence to which the laughter is attached. When laughter happens at the end of the sentence, I prefer to place [*laughter*] before the period; this makes it clear that the speaker laughs at the previous statement and that they are not laughing at what you or they are going to say next. If laughter happens at the beginning of the sentence, I place [*laughs*] at the beginning of the sentence and after the preceding sentence's period. I did not always include laughter, but I started giving an indication for laughter after my first few interviews. Tone can be difficult to convey, pick up, and interpret strictly from the text. We interpret body language and the actual sounds, rhythms, and shifts in a particular person's voice to help determine meaning. Although infrequent, notes such as [voice goes up], [sarcastically], [sadly], [hesitantly], and so forth do appear in interviews, along with notes on physical motions if the interview is in-person or conducted via video. While there is nothing wrong with including these sorts of indicators, they can be distracting and the interview can read more like a screenplay or script. Another problem with these indicators is that they demonstrate an instance of telling versus showing. The person's words should do the work of showing the emotion. If you do use them, I would advise keeping them to a minimum and placing those sorts of notes when they are either particularly impactful (e.g., a sudden and drastic shift in tone or mood) or the emotional tone of the words is unclear.

You may have to or have the option to write an introduction for the interview. If so, you can include details and information about setting tone, mood, the feel or vibe that you got while talking with the interviewee, and the interviewee's general demeanor.

Small Talk

I tend to eliminate opening and closing small talk such as "Hello. How are you?" and "Thank you for the interview" from the final version of the interview. I still perform, initiate, and respond to these important and customary civilities in the interview; I just don't include them in the final form. I cut them for the same reason television shows and movies usually don't show characters putting on their shoes and socks, grabbing their wallets and purses, and locking the door before they leave: It's not very interesting, it doesn't add anything to the story, and we can assume those actions take place. However, I follow the model of whatever publication I happen to be writing for. Some publications tend to include that sort of material so if they do it, then I do it. I wouldn't say it's strictly wrong to include small talk.

Ways to Turn the Audio into Text Other Than Typing It Yourself

After you have decided whom you want to interview, researched their career, gotten them to agree to an interview, constructed questions, and conducted the interview, there is still the actual rendering of the interview into a publishable piece. There are shortcuts and ways to make that less difficult, but there really is no easy way to hammer the thing onto the page. The closest thing to an automatic process is to pay a transcription service to transcribe the interview for you. I don't have any opinions on any companies I suggest using or avoiding because I don't have any experience using any of them. I briefly investigated their services a couple of years ago and decided against using them, mainly because I didn't want to pay. My recollection is that some of them offer free trials or so many free minutes per month, so you can experiment without too much investment. A note of caution: If you use one of these services, you still need to review the printed interview for several reasons. You need to check for accuracy because the final responsibility rests with you. Also, I don't think I have ever sent in an interview that I did not make some sort of change to. As we will talk about, producing a good interview requires skillful and deliberate editing. A transcription service is either not going to do any sort of editing for you or it will be at a very minimal level, so expect to perform further work on the interview yourself after the service returns it to you, or prepare to pay for an editing service to handle that phase. As we have begun to see, editing is not always about right/wrong decisions. An editing service is probably not going to make stylistic and aesthetic decisions about, for example, organization and deletion of material.

You may also find some free services, apps, or programs online or in your computer. Google Docs is one. Once you open a blank document, click on "Tools" and then "Voice Typing." From there, you speak into your microphone and Google Docs transforms your spoken words into words on the page. Programs and features are always changing, but when I was using it there were certain short-cuts available like saying "period" when you want to end a sentence with a period. I've read accounts that Google Docs may auto-punctuate for you and may add punctuation when you don't want it. My general experience was that using Google Docs was not as simple as just talking out loud. I couldn't talk too fast, it often rendered words and phrases incorrectly, and even when I deleted out the wrong part and repeated myself, sometimes it still rendered my words incorrectly. All in all, I don't think I saved or spent any additional time transcribing; it just was a different process. However, if you type slowly, using Google Docs might speed up your transcription, especially if you have very clear enunciation. The main advantage for me was that it gave my fingers and arms a chance to rest. When I was typing well over a thousand words every day, week after week, I began to experience some pain in my wrists and forearms at night. This is always a sign to cut back and let the body recover. Using Google Docs let me continue to make progress but took some of the strain off of my limbs. By the way, I had a brief fantasy that maybe I could place the voice recorder close to Google Docs, let it run, come back when the tape had played through, and find my interview magically transcribed. However, after trying this for a few minutes, I found that Google Docs didn't pick anything up.

Windows 11 (the current version of Windows as of this writing) also has a voice typing feature, which I experimented with after recently buying a completely new computer. If I use Google Docs, I have to cut and paste material from there into Microsoft Word. With Windows, I can perform voice typing directly into Word. I feel Windows 11 does at least a good a job as Google Docs, maybe better. Since I don't use Google Docs for anything else, I'd probably use Window's voice typing feature since I can input material straight into the file.

If you can pay for a voice typing program, Kurzweil 3000 is a brand of learning-assistive software. Among its many features, Kurzweil has a speech-to-text function. You can get a free trial through the website, see how it works for you, find current pricing, and decide if it's worth buying.

My prediction is any of these systems will get better and better at voice typing with each release and update, allowing you to transcribe by voice with fewer mistakes and more efficiency. If you don't like voice typing now, try again when there's a new upgrade to whatever program you tried. I'm not completely sold yet, but every time I try or retry one of these methods, I like it more.

Typing the Interview Yourself

If you are not going to use a professional service or a speech-to-text program, then you are transcribing by hand from the recorder. I've talked about this before in the section about picking a recorder, but it merits a quick recap. Get a decent recorder that is easy to use, has large enough buttons, won't break down or fail to operate at critical moments, and has some basic features. Be sure your recorder can fast forward and rewind at a speedy clip so that you are not spending unneeded time trying to get to a specific point in the interview. Some recorders are compatible with certain foot pedals, which will allow you to rewind, stop, and fast forward without taking your hands off of the keyboard, picking up the recorder, stopping/rewinding/fast forwarding, putting the recorder back down, and resuming typing. I don't have any familiarity with foot pedals, but I mention them should you want to investigate that option. I sometimes play back the recording while listening to it through earbuds or headphones. If the recording is clear, I don't need it, but if the recording, or parts of it, are hard to hear, someone else is in your space and wants to hear something besides your taped interview, or you are in a public space, headphones or earbuds come in handy. The ability to control the rate of playback is also important. Generally, I play the tape back at normal speed and stop it when I need to catch up or can't make out a word or phrase. I've tried slowing the tape down to a rate that I can keep up with, but I end up stopping anyway. Slowing down the tape, however, has been useful when I need to isolate a word, usually a name, that I can't quite hear clearly enough. If you are fast on the keyboard, you might even want to speed the tape up.

I've also tried several methods of transcribing. One technique I used is to just let the recording play at its normal rate, catch what I can as it passes by, and then go through the tape again from start to finish to catch what I missed. While that method makes each individual *pass* easier, it complicates the overall process and takes more time. Even making just a second pass creates a deficit. You may, of course, be different, but what is most efficient for me is to make one pass at a normal playback speed, pausing the tape when I need to catch up, and going back over individual words or passages as needed by either pausing the tape or slowing down specific words or passages. For me, give or take on average, ten minutes of tape takes me about an hour to transcribe. Thus, a thirty-minute interview will take me about three hours to make a complete initial draft. Add in the time to get in touch with the interviewee and set the interview up, researching and making questions, and conducting the interview and I'm up to about five or six hours of time spent on that "short" thirty-minute interview. Again, this is just to develop a working draft. Doing it right takes time, and you can only work so quickly.

First Draft Example: Pete Von Sholly

If we consider setting up and getting ready for the interview by doing our research and making our questions as the first step and conducting the interview as the second step, then making a first full draft is our next step.

Now, we'll take a look at a first draft that skips the verbatim stage by eliminating filler words and most of the false starts. This draft resembles an intelligent verbatim draft. You'll see times noted in parentheses beside certain passages and at other points. This is so that I can find or get close to a particular place on tape in case I need to review it. Sometimes a time appears when I ask a new question. Sometimes I just put the time in every so often. Sometimes I put it in whenever I stop for the day or take a break so that I can easily find where I left off when I turn the recorder back on. These small organizational steps I advise taking—making folders, labelling files, putting in timestamps—may seem like unnecessary busywork, but they are useful and save time and energy.

If you are interested and have not already read it, the "Spontaneous Interviews" section give the backstory for the following interview.

*

Please talk about your involvement and what you did with The Fantastic Four.

I did all the storyboards for the special effects and the stunts. Things like that. I didn't work one-on-one with the director. Different directors work different ways. He basically just trusted me with most of it, so I went with it. I took the ball and . . . Sometimes they want your ideas and input; sometimes they want to tell you exactly what to do. He was pretty easy to work with that way. What else can I tell you?

(:44) *How many storyboards did you make?*

I have no idea. Many pages worth. All the effects sequences where somebody would stretch or transform, flame on, and things like that.

What kind of feedback did you get?

They seemed pleased with what I did. There was not a lot of nitpicking. There were times when I felt that once we'd seen Ben Grimm turn into the Thing, seeing it again is kind of needlessly expensive. I knew the budget was tight, so I did one shot where you're looking at his shadow and the shadow transforms. We know what's happening, but we see it that way, which I thought was a way to show variety in how the transformation happens and to make it more interesting visually. I don't remember exactly. Oley was fine with all that kind of stuff.

(1:56) *So for that scene, you show it in full once and then there were other ways to suggest or represent it a little less expensively.*

Yeah. I just thought also it would be more visually interesting. They didn't have CG effects to play with very freely. What year was the movie?

They were shooting it at the very end of 1992. Post-production, such as there was for the film, would have been 1993.

Right. That was when *Jurassic Park* came out. So CG was sort of new and expensive, so it wasn't an option for them, I don't think, except maybe the Human Torch. They might have had some crude CG for the Torch.

(2:43) *What was the process for making the storyboards? Did you look at the screenplay and then adapt images from that or how did this work?*

Yeah. You go through the script and look for sequences and scenes that require storyboarding. Storyboards are useful for the production people because you can imagine a thing many different ways. Not everything is explained just because it says on a page that somebody walks into a room and fires a gun. Okay, well, how does that work?

You could shoot that a hundred different ways. Once there's a storyboard of it, then everybody involved can look at that and go, "Oh, okay. I see what the director wants. I see what we need to do." So that's kind of the purpose of it. A lot of times they don't have the time or the budget to storyboard the whole movie, and so I would say to directors, "Well, what are your priority sequences? Maybe make the shots that absolutely need storyboarding and make that your A-list. If we finish that and have time, do you have a B-list?" Some directors don't use much storyboarding or some don't use it at all, and some like to use it a lot. It depends on how much time and budget there is as to whether a film can have somebody like me on staff.

(4:07) So besides the transformation of Ben Grimm to the Thing what are some other things you can recall that you storyboarded for the movie?

When Reed would stretch, anything involving the Torch, anything involving special effects of any kind.

When you make that storyboard, that common visual reference for everyone, is that what everybody including the special effects team and the director refers to?

Yeah. I storyboarded a lot of movies in those years and in the 1980s a lot of *A Nightmare on Elm Street* movies, *Darkman* for Sam Raimi, and stuff like that. Once the storyboards are drawn, everybody starts referring to them. Even the sets can use storyboards. If you're storyboarding a scene that takes place in a room but the camera is only looking in one direction, maybe you don't need to build the whole room, or maybe you don't need to dress the whole room. If Reed needs to stretch, then what's he have to do? Does he have to reach out to pick something up? Is it just him stretching? What is required? A storyboard lets everybody down the line know what their responsibilities are. It changes. Things change a lot from the storyboard stage. Sometimes things come out just like you storyboarded them, and sometimes they come out really, really different for a variety of reasons.

Are there any other examples of that that you can remember from the movie?

No, I'm not that familiar with the finished film

I was and am a big fan of Jack Kirby. To me that's the Fantastic Four, so it was really fun to do the movie and draw those characters and stuff, but other than that there isn't anything that stands out about this from any other movie, except for the fact that it involved these cool characters that I grew up with.

Some directors like to sit together with you and go through a sequence shot-by-shot and say, "Okay, I want to open with a wide shot, or a medium two-shot of these two people. Then I want a high wide angle of then. Then I want to boom down and push in on them." So you sort of figure it out beat-by-beat that way. Other times they turn you loose because they're busy, or they want your input so you get to kind of play director sometimes. In this case, I just remember having a lot of freedom and Oley liking what I did. I wish I had more specific memories and could tell you more. I know you're going to hear this a lot but it was a long time ago.

I storyboarded a lot of films. You're interested just in this Roger Corman film, I assume?

Yes sir, primarily.

Okay. I ask because I worked on another version of it that didn't get made years later. Raja Gosnell was going to direct it. He directed the *Scooby-Doo* movie and some other things. There was another version of *The Fantastic Four* that we did a lot of work on, but it didn't happen for some reason. That's a whole different thing, right?

(8:10) It's not the central focus but that's stuff I can use images from and we can talk about also. Sure.

Let me give you my email. Send me an e-mail, and I'll see if I can find any images to attach.

(8:35) So what happened with that version? This would have been after the unreleased Corman version but before the 2005 one that finally came out.

Yeah. It might have been Fox that was going to do it. I could tell that they didn't really understand the characters. They talked about the Thing like he was the Rock Guy, like he's made out of rock. I understand that you could look at him and he think he looks kind of like that, but he's not made out of rocks. Jack Kirby actually told me once that the Thing is like a gorilla covered in dinosaur hide, so it's a scaly texture. It's organic. It's not rocks. So some of the concept designs people were putting crystals on the Thing and stuff like that trying to play with the idea that it was rocks. I was just shaking my head thinking, "That's not right" [*laughs*]. They were redesigning everything. It was just stupid stuff going on. I don't know why they ended up not making the movie, but I think it's just as well. They still haven't made a good *Fantastic Four* movie.

You actually met Jack Kirby, then?

A few times over the years. Yeah.

Tell me about him. What was he like? What else did he tell you about the Fantastic Four?

(10:01) Nothing about the Fantastic Four. He was a wonderful, polite, welcoming, gentle man. I went to his house a few times. His wife Roz would always welcome you and maybe give you a tuna fish sandwich and a cup of coffee or something. You were always treated like guests even if you were someone that had only met them at conventions and things. I bought a couple of pieces of original art from him over the years, so I went over and visited them. I was not what I would call a close friend of the family or anything like that. Roz usually handled the invitations and all of that. Jack was Jack sitting there doing comics. You'll never hear a bad thing about Jack from all the people who knew him, met him, and worked with him. He was always encouraging. What he always encouraged you to do was find you own style. Don't copy his style. Find your own style. Be yourself. He always had a good thing to say. Just the nicest man you'd ever want to know.

Did you ever meet Stan Lee?

I did. I worked at Marvel Animation for a while. Stan had an office there. I grew up reading *Fantastic Four*, so Stan and Jack were important to me. I didn't know the ins and outs. You know it's controversial about who did what, the credit and compensation, and all that. I didn't know anything about that. I just knew that when I grew up, I wanted to be Stan Lee and Jack Kirby because I wanted to write and draw comics. For me, those guy were big inspirations for that kind of comic. You could go into Stan's office and say hello to him. He knew who I was and I would visit. I was doing drawings and he would critique the drawings if I asked. He was very lively and friendly. He would jump around and strike poses. He would say, "Well, look. In this drawing here, you should do this or try that." He seemed like he appreciated the fact that there were people who knew who he, Kirby, Ditko, and all of the Marvel comics makers were. They were important to people. He was not aloof or unfriendly at all . . . to me, anyway. It was just a special thing to meet both of those guys. I was like, "Wow! These are the guys I grew up with, and here they are." You can actually . . . Your heroes are real human beings. You can meet them and talk to them. It's very cool.

Yeah.

(13:05) Steve Ditko passed away recently. You mentioned his name. Did you have interaction with him?

No. I didn't. I called him up once. When I was a kid, I was in New York at my Grandma's house on Flushing, Long Island. She had a phonebook that I was looking at, and there's his name, Steve Ditko. I called him up and he answered. What are going to say? "First of all, I didn't think you'd answer the phone. Is it really you?"

He goes, "Oh, yeah. Yeah." He was still doing *Spider-Man* at that time. I just said some stupid stuff like, "Gee, you're great. I love your work" [*laughs*]. He was very friendly. He didn't say, "Don't bother me." I didn't get an unfriendly vibe. He seemed to just take it in stride because his phone number is listed, so people are going to call him up. That was it. I just got the impression of him as a friendly guy.

Marvel had offices on Madison Avenue in those days in the 1960s. My older brother took me there one day. He said, "Let's go see if we can meet Stan Lee." He didn't care. He said, "Well there's the address; let's just go up." We went up and saw Flo Steinberg—who was this wonderful lady—who was Stan's secretary for many years. You might have heard of her.

She has a very interesting story in her own right.

Yes, she does. She came out into the reception room. She said, "Hi. Stan is busy. I'm sorry you can't meet him. What can I do for you?" I had this little shitty comic book that I had drawn, and I thought. "Gee, I bet Stan will like this." As a kid you don't have a clue as to whether what you did is actually any good or not, or else you're in denial about the fact that it's just amateur work. That's a blessing because it allows you to keep going and not get discouraged. She said, "We can't take things from outside sources. Good for you. Keep working." She was very sweet, but I didn't get in the office. I had the feeling from reading Stan's letters page that there was the bullpen and Steve Ditko, Jack Kirby, and everybody else were all in there working together, talking, and it was this big group. It wasn't like that really, but that's the way Stan made it sound. I tried to go see him. Like I said I ended up working at the same place many years later, so it did come around.

(16:14) Right. Did you save that little comic book that you had made up?

Somewhere. Somewhere I have it. I think I have it. It's just awful, though.

What was it about?

It was a superhero named Nerve Master. I guess I was the one with a lot of nerve [*laughs*]. The character could control your nervous system, so he could make you think that you heard things and saw things that you didn't. I tried. It was just a few pages. When you're a kid, in those days at least, you didn't know that comic artists drew the pages bigger. You just saw the printed page and assumed that you had to draw it that size. My stuff was drawn on eight and a half inch by eleven inch paper. Just tiny. You think, "How do they do this? This is really small." Then later on you find out that's not how they do it.

But I always loved *Fantastic Four*. Growing up that was one of my favorite comics, so getting to work on a couple of movie versions of it was great fun. Anytime you're drawing *Spider-Man*, *Superman*, or *The Fantastic Four*, whatever, professionally, you stop to think, "*Damn*. This is cool."

(17:52) What is it about the Fantastic Four? Why do you like them so much?

Because of Jack Kirby, really. You know when I read those now, sometimes the dialogue is kind of ridiculous. They don't hold up that well for me, but the artwork does. Kirby's creativity is on another level. It looked to me like Kirby always wanted to entertain himself, and he wanted to have a good time. He would always start an issue off with this really strong visual to get you interested and get you excited and get you into the story. He has a really good sense of "What would I want to see? What would I think is cool?" and that came across. Then, there was that period when he was creating the Silver Surfer and Black Panther, which was just amazing. And Thor. At that same time, the *Thor* comic book was introducing all these incredible, new characters and they were in outer space and all sorts of places. Jack was really on a roll, creatively. It was exciting because this was all brand-new stuff. Now, there's thousands of issues of all these books. There's so much history, but in those days it was all pretty new. Every time the new Marvel comics came out—especially during the heyday of Ditko and Kirby—it was only so many, so everything that they did was fresh and exciting.

(19:39) So how did you get involved with the film?

I don't remember who referred me, but a lot of storyboard jobs get referred. You work on a movie and somebody there maybe likes what you did, so they get another movie and they say, "Hey, I met a guy that was a good storyboard guy. If you're looking for a guy, here's his information." The phone would ring and they'd say, "We're looking for a storyboard artist. Are you interested?" You say, "yes," and they send you a script, usually. You read the script and you're supposed to tell them if you're interested or not. I got one script that I thought was awful. I thought, "Jeez, what am I gonna say about this?" The producer called me up and asked, "Did you get the script?" I said, "Yeah." She said, "Well, what'd you think? People either love or they hate it. Which were *you*?" I said, "I hated it, actually." She said, "Does that mean you don't want to work on it?" I said, "*No*, it doesn't mean I don't want to work on it. I'll do my best to do what I'm supposed to do, but you asked." They hired me and I worked on it, so they didn't hold it against me because I was honest.

What film was that?

Heathers. Winona Ryder. Christian Slater. The movie was actually a lot better than I thought it would be from reading the script. The script just didn't appeal to me for some reason. I read the script for the first *Buffy the Vampire Slayer* movie, and I did not get that job, but the script was great.

To answer your question, it was usually word of mouth and referrals where jobs would come from. I liked the *Evil Dead* movies, and I read in *Fangoria* or some place that Sam Raimi was making *Darkman*, and I thought, "Man, I'd like to work on that," so I called Tony Gardner, the effects guy. I had known him and worked with him. He was working on *Darkman* and he told me to call Universal and ask for Sam Raimi. I called and they just put me through! I told his secretary I wanted to work on the film, she arranged a meeting, and I got hired. Sometimes you can aggressively go after something like that. Other times, you work for a director and they like what you did, so they hire you again. Then, there's a connection.

(22:56) Did you ever meet Roger Corman?

Only once, just to say hello. I think I had a meeting with him once. I don't even remember why. I think I was trying to pitch him a project or something. He was nice. He was friendly. Nothing happened.

(23:27) Do you have anything else that comes to mind?

(23:38) I wish I could tell you more about that specific movie. I would say one thing about storyboarding for people who don't know what it is. You start with a script, and you end up with a movie. Somewhere right in the middle is the storyboard. The storyboard is the point where the script becomes visible. You get the director's vision down on paper, and then everybody knows what he wants. The storyboard artist can have a lot of creative input and a lot of influence on things, or very little depending on the director's receptivity.

[Discussion about what I was doing with this interview and the history of the project.]

(26:15) I brought in Kirby comics and Kirby artwork to Oley Sassone. He liked it. I think he knew he didn't have the budget and could only get so much on the screen. I do have the sense that he liked and respected the material. That's just my impression of what he was like. He wanted to honor the comics and what was good about the comics the best he could with the budget and so forth.

I spoke with him, and that's the impression that I had gotten that he really wanted to try to be faithful to the comics. It's one of the things I've heard, too, from a lot of people that the unreleased version is the one that's more faithful to the comic books, and I would agree with that.

(27:31) I worked at Disney Imagineering for a few years also, for eight years, and I did a lot of stuff for them involving the Marvel characters for theme parks and things like that. That was another case of getting to draw Spider-Man, Captain America, Iron Man, and everybody. All ideas for park attractions, things that you could do and play in parks now that they have Marvel. There was going to be a Doctor Strange ride and stuff like that. It was so much fun to storyboard Doctor Strange and what the ride would be like. That was another thing where I can't believe I'm getting paid to draw Doctor Strange and these characters that I grew up with *[laughs]*. I don't think most of those things got made. You develop things and illustrate them and go through the process. Some things come out the other end and some things don't. I don't know what become of any of that stuff. It's all kind of secret. They wanted to do theme park things for Marvel. Getting to draw those characters was such a treat for a guy like me.

(28:53) I know there's the Incredible Hulk one and we went on it a few years ago. Do you recall if you did any of the stuff for that ride?

I did stuff involving the Hulk, but it's hard to say what happened to it. If it got used or not.

But it might have?

It might have.

It's always fun to talk to people who love this kind of stuff because it's been a real treat of a job and a career to be involved in moviemaking, particularly when they're good, which they're not always.

Thank you, so much.

[Discussion of release forms, sending him a transcription, time-lines, and so forth.]

Second Draft Example Including Corrections, Edits, and Revisions: Pete Von Sholly

The next step is turning that first draft example into a final polished and publishable piece. This is where the art and craft of writing really begin to come into play. Decisions may be less about right and wrong and more about what looks and sounds better stylistically. We want to take the interview from good to great.

In this version, I take the first pass from the previous section and show you all of the edits I made. Strikethroughs show content I edited out. Bolded content with brackets shows content I added in. Explanatory notes are also bolded in brackets and begin with "note." I use the notes to tell you why I made certain changes, what I was thinking at the time, and, here and there, what I might do differently if I were edited the interview now. Usually, the note refers to content preceding the note, but occasionally it seemed better to reverse the order. I wouldn't put it on the page this way with brackets, striketh-roughs, and so on; I would just make the changes in the next draft. For our purposes, I went through and reverse-engineered the final draft to pinpoint and show you the changes I decided on. Basically, you'll see three types of changes. There are places where I add, eliminate, or change individual words. There are places where I strike out—and occasionally add—sentences and phrases. There are also places where I move sentences or paragraphs from one section of the interview to another in order to make it read or flow better. Generally, I feel more comfortable tinkering with my words than the interviewee's. I sometimes use my questions as a space to include information useful to the reader—kind of like a footnote—that may not have been a part of the actual interview, so if I insert something that was not originally said, I almost always tend to add it to my words. I do not ever twist someone else's words or change the basic meaning of what someone says, but this third kind of revision in which I may move sentences or paragraphs around is a delicate pro-cess. If you do it, be careful that you stay true to the content, mean-ing, and spirit of the interviewee's actual words.

I feel comfortable with this kind of intensive editing for two reasons. I have taught writing at the collegiate level for over two decades, so I feel I understand and am sensitive to nuances and shades of meaning with language. Also, since I offer to let interviewees read and revise their interview, I feel better about making larger sorts of changes. If you do not feel comfortable performing that level of editing, then don't do it. If you don't plan on letting the interviewee look at the interview before publication—my understanding is that usually interviewees are not offered this opportunity—you might err on the conservative side when moving content around. However, I would still remove the speech fillers, eliminate the false starts and repetitive content, and smooth out or correct grammar and syntax. Those edits are virtually undebatable, easy to edit, and flat transcription can be tedious to read and unflattering to both interviewer and interviewee.

I think of producing the final version of the interview as more like making an objective documentary as compared to a reality television show. Even in a documentary, not all of the footage appears. Producers and others edit, sequence, choose, and mix content for albums, television, and films. Unless, the movie is a continuous shot of live and unbroken footage from a single camera, there is some editing and selection involved, and that's without even getting into the idea of adding voiceovers, music, explanatory text on the screen, narration, and any kind of separate introduction and conclusion. However, I do not edit in such a way as to change the basic content and meaning. As we know, reality television producers may edit footage in a manner that creates two-dimensional characters rather than presents three-dimensional people. For example, there exists the theory of the "villain edit" in which footage and words are heavily edited in such a way as to create and frame someone as a villain. Another technique is the "franken-bite," a process in which the postproduction crew sifts through hours of footage to stitch together and create sound bites that the speaker never said. We could argue that the "hero edit" exists as well in which a person or team edits someone else's words or footage to make them appear softer, more capable, nicer, better than how they would otherwise appear. This, too, is a misrepresentation. I correct, I edit, I revise. I polish. I do not manipulate or distort. I present.

Here is the transitional, marked up draft between the first pass and final version of the Pete Von Sholly interview:

[A note before we get too far into this. The *The* is a little tricky. When I was going through the entire interview collection, I researched and discovered that for the first fifteen issues, the comic was named *The Fantastic Four*. Beginning with issue #16, *the* was dropped and the title became *Fantastic Four*. The Corman movie is titled *The Fantastic Four* and all of the subsequent films to date are *Fantastic Four*. Usually, it's obvious which movie an interviewee references and whether *The* is required. Other times, I didn't know but asked for clarification. When the distinction was not so important, I just made a decision during the editing process. For example, we can't hear the difference between "I enjoyed *The Fantastic Four* comic" and "I enjoyed the *Fantastic Four* comic" or "I like the Fantastic Four" (referring to the team) and "I like *The Fantastic Four*" (referring to the comic).]

Pete Von Sholly (Storyboard Artist) **[note: I use the interviewee's entire name and a brief explanation in parentheses of his involvement with the film.]**

Please talk about your involvement and what you did with The Fantastic Four.

I did all the storyboards for the special effects ~~and~~ **[,]**the stunts. **[,and]** ~~T~~**[t]**hings like that. I didn't work one-on-one with the director. Different directors work different ways. He **[Oley] [note: If this was a standalone interview, I would provide Oley Sassone's full name and insert something about him being the director of *The Fantastic Four*. As this interview appears in a larger collection, and Sassone has a separate interview, I felt that identifying him by first name would be suffice.]** basically just trusted me with most of it, so I went with it. ~~I took the ball and . . .~~ Sometimes they want your ideas and input; sometimes they want to tell you exactly what to do. He was pretty easy to work with that way. ~~What else can I tell you?~~

(:44) *How many storyboards did you make?*

I have no idea **[exactly] [note: Looking back on it now, I probably wouldn't add "exactly" because I am not sure it really adds value or clarifies anything.]** Many pages worth. All the effects sequences where somebody would stretch or transform, flame on, and things like that.

What kind of feedback did you get?

They seemed pleased with what I did. There was not a lot of nitpicking. There were times when I felt that once we'd seen Ben Grimm turn into the Thing, seeing it again is **[was] [note: I am trying to keep the verb tenses somewhat consistent.]** kind of needlessly expensive. I knew the budget was tight, so I did one shot where you're looking at his shadow and the shadow transforms. We know what's happening, but we see it that way, which I thought was a way to show variety in how the transformation happens and to make it more interesting visually. ~~I don't remember exactly.~~ Oley was fine with all that kind of stuff.

(1:56) *So for that scene, you show it in full once and then there were other ways to suggest or represent it a little less expensively.*

Yeah. I just thought also it would be more visually interesting. They didn't have CG effects to play with very freely. What year was the movie?

They were shooting it at the very end of 1992. Post-production, ~~such as there was for the film,~~ would have been 1993.

Right. That was when *Jurassic Park* came out. So CG was sort of new and expensive, so it wasn't an option for them, I don't think, except maybe the Human Torch. They might have had some crude CG **[available]** for the Torch.

(2:43) *What was the process for making the storyboards? Did you look at the screenplay and then adapt images from that or how did this work?*

Yeah. You go through the script and look for sequences and scenes that require storyboarding. Storyboards are useful for the production people because you can imagine a thing many different ways. Not everything is explained just because it says on a page that somebody walks into a room and fires a gun. Okay, well, how does that work?

You could shoot that a hundred different ways. Once there's a storyboard of it, then everybody involved can look at that and go, "Oh, okay. I see what the director wants. I see what we need to do." So that's kind of the purpose of it. A lot of times they don't have the time or the budget to storyboard the whole movie, and so I would say to directors, "Well, what are your priority sequences? Maybe make the shots that absolutely need storyboarding and make that your A-list. If we finish that and have time, do you have a B-list?" Some directors don't use much storyboarding or some don't use it at all, and some like to use it a lot. It depends on how much time and budget there is as to whether a film can have somebody like me on staff.

~~*(4:07) So besides the transformation of Ben Grimm to the Thing what are some other things you can recall that you storyboarded for the movie?*~~

~~When Reed would stretch, anything involving the Torch, anything involving special effects of any kind.~~

When you make that storyboard, that common visual reference for everyone, is that what everybody including the special effects team and the director refers to?

Yeah. I storyboarded a lot of movies in those years and in the 1980s a lot of *A Nightmare on Elm Street* movies, *Darkman* for Sam Raimi, and stuff like that. Once the storyboards are drawn, everybody starts referring to them. ~~Even the sets can use storyboards.~~ **[Storyboards can even help with designing the sets.]** If you're storyboarding a scene that takes place in a room but the camera is only looking in one direction, maybe you don't need to build the whole room, or maybe you don't need to dress the whole room. If Reed needs to stretch, then what's he have to do? Does he have to reach out to pick something up? Is it just him stretching? What is required? A storyboard lets everybody down the line know what their responsibilities are. It changes. Things change a lot from the storyboard stage. Sometimes things come out just like you storyboarded them, and sometimes they come out really, really different for a variety of reasons.

Are there any other examples of that that you can remember from the movie?

No, I'm not that familiar with the finished film.

~~I was and am a big fan of Jack Kirby. To me that's the Fantastic Four,~~ **[note: I move this to form a part of the answer to the upcoming question about Sholly meeting Jack Kirby.]** ~~so it was really fun to do the movie and draw those characters and stuff,~~ **[note: I move this to the end of the interview.]** ~~but other than that there isn't anything that stands out about this from any other movie, except for the fact that it involved these cool characters that I grew up with.~~

Some directors like to sit ~~together~~ with you and go through a sequence shot-by-shot and say, "Okay, I want to open with a wide shot, or a medium two-shot of these two people. Then I want a high, wide angle of them. Then I want to boom down and push in on them." So you sort of figure it out beat-by-beat that way. Other times they turn you loose because they're busy, or they want your input so you get to kind of play director ~~sometimes~~ **[for a minute]**. In this case, I just remember having a lot of freedom and Oley liking what I did. I wish I had more specific memories and could tell you more. I know you're going to hear this a lot but it was a long time ago. **[note: This is as good a place as any to discuss how to break up the sentences into paragraphs. Sometimes it's just time for a break; one answer should not run as an unbroken paragraph for pages and pages. Other times, like this one, the answer begins to shift topics, and so starting a new paragraph makes sense.]**

I storyboarded a lot of films. You're interested just in this Roger Corman film, I assume?

Yes sir, primarily.

Okay. I ask because I worked on another version of it that didn't get made years later. Raja Gosnell was going to direct it. He directed the *Scooby-Doo* movie and some other things. There was another version of *The Fantastic Four* that we did a lot of work on, but it didn't happen for some reason. ~~That's a whole different thing, right?~~

~~*(8:10) It's not the central focus but that's stuff I can use images from and we can talk about also. Sure.*~~

~~Let me give you my email. Send me an e-mail, and I'll see if I can find any images to attach.~~

(8:35) So what happened with that version? This would have been after the unreleased Corman version but before the 2005 one that finally came out.

Yeah. It might have been Fox that was going to do it. I could tell that they didn't really understand the characters. They talked about the Thing like he was the Rock Guy, like he's **[actually]** made out of rock. I understand that you could look at him and he think he looks kind of like that, but he's not made out of rocks. Jack Kirby actually told me once that the Thing is like a gorilla covered in dinosaur hide, so it's a scaly texture. It's organic. It's not rocks. So **[In]** some of the concept designs people were putting crystals on the Thing and stuff like that trying to play with the idea that it was rocks. I was just shaking my head thinking, "That's not right" [*laughs*]. They were redesigning everything. It was just stupid stuff going on. I don't know why they ended up not making the movie, but I think it's just as well. They still haven't made a good *Fantastic Four* movie.

[note: Although this is sequenced in the book as an early interview, I actually conducted it about halfway through the

cycle. At this point of the overall process, I realized that most of the people I talked with weren't connected with the actual people from Marvel. Moving Sholly towards talking about some of those people would cover some ground no one else really had or could. If we had gotten off on a tangent about, say, baseball, I wouldn't have included much, if any, of that in the interview; I love baseball, but it's just not relevant. However, I think people reading about this movie are also interested in the creators of the Fantastic Four and Marvel Comics. As the interview reveals, Sholly shared personal and professional interactions with more people than Kirby. I also started to feel that Sholly had told me all about Corman's *The Fantastic Four* as he could and pushing further in that direction wasn't going to take us anywhere new. Although I had enough for a short but complete interview, I didn't get the sense that Sholly wanted to stop talking; he just didn't have anything else to say about *The Fantastic Four*.]

You actually met Jack Kirby, then?

A few times over the years. ~~Yeah.~~ **[I was and am a big fan of Jack Kirby. To me that's the Fantastic Four] [note: As discussed, this comes from an earlier section that I moved here.]**

Tell me about him. What was he like? What else did he tell you about the Fantastic Four?

(10:01) Nothing about the Fantastic Four. He was a wonderful, polite, welcoming, gentle man. I went to his house a few times. His wife Roz would always welcome you and maybe give you a tuna fish sandwich and a cup of coffee or something. You were always treated like guests even if you were someone that had only met them at conventions and things. I bought a couple of pieces of original art from him over the years, so I went over and visited them. I was not what I would call a close friend of the family or anything like that. Roz usually handled the invitations and all of that. Jack was Jack sitting there doing comics. You'll never hear a bad thing about Jack from all the people who knew him, met him, and worked with him. He was always encouraging. What he always encouraged you to do was find you own style. Don't copy his style. Find your own style. Be yourself. He always had a good thing to say. **[and was]** J[j]ust the nicest man you'd ever want to know.

[note: That was enlightening. Sholly does a really good job of creating a scene, almost as if he is storyboarding in words one of his visits to the Kirby household. You can't tell as much

from the printed interview as you can from the recording, but Sholly's tone changed. He sounded excited and seemed to enjoy reminiscing about these folks. At this point, I decided to ask him about some of the other big Marvel names. Even if he hadn't known any of them, he might still have something good to say.]

Did you ever meet Stan Lee?

I did. I worked at Marvel Animation for a while. Stan had an office there. I grew up reading *The Fantastic Four*, so Stan and Jack were important to me. I didn't know the ins and outs. You know it's controversial about who did what, the credit and compensation, and all that. I didn't know anything about that. I just knew that when I grew up, I wanted to be Stan Lee and Jack Kirby because I wanted to write and draw comics. For me, those guy were big inspirations for that kind of comic. You could go into Stan's office and say hello to him. He knew who I was and I would visit. I was doing drawings and he would critique ~~the drawings~~ **[them]** if I asked. He was very lively and friendly. He would jump around and strike poses. He would say, "Well, look. In this drawing here, you should do this or try that." He seemed like he appreciated the fact that there were people who knew who he, Kirby, Ditko, and all of the Marvel comics makers were. They were important to people. He was not aloof or unfriendly at all . . . to me, anyway. It was just a special thing to meet both of those guys. I was like, "Wow! These are the guys I grew up with, and here they are." ~~You can actually . . .~~ Your heroes are real human beings. You can meet them and talk to them. It's very cool.

~~Yeah.~~ **[note: I cut this. I was enthusiastically agreeing with Sholly, but *yeah* can also sound very flat and disinterested, kind of like *uh-huh*. People sometimes use an exclamation mark to try to convey a sense of excitement, but we should not rely on those. They can be easy to overuse and once overused lose their power.]**

(13:05) ~~*Steve Ditko*~~ ***[He]*** *passed away recently. You mentioned* ~~*his name*~~ ***[Steve Ditko]***. **[note: I reversed the order of the previous two sentences for the final version.]** *Did you have **[any]** interaction with him?*

No. I didn't. I called him up once. When I was a kid, I was in New York at my Grandma's house on Flushing, Long Island. She had a phonebook that I was looking at, and there's his name, Steve

Ditko. I called him up and he answered. What are going to say? "First of all, I didn't think you'd answer the phone. Is it really you?" He goes, "Oh, yeah. Yeah." He was still doing *Spider-Man* at that time. I just said some stupid stuff like, "Gee, you're great. I love your work" [*laughs*]. He was very friendly. He didn't say, "Don't bother me." I didn't get an unfriendly vibe. He seemed to just take it in stride because his phone number is listed, so people are going to call him up. That was it. I just got the impression of him as a friendly guy.

Marvel had offices on Madison Avenue in those days in the 1960s. My older brother took me there one day. He said, "Let's go see if we can meet Stan Lee." ~~He didn't care. He said, "Well there's the address; let's just go up."~~ We went up and saw Flo Steinberg— who was this wonderful lady—who was Stan's secretary for many years. You might have heard of her.

"Fabulous" Flo. She did a lot things at Marvel. Left Marvel, came back, and in between published Big Apple Comix. Her name doesn't come up in comics as much as some others, but [S]she has a very interesting story in her own right.

[note: In truth, I had not heard of her. I didn't want to break the flow of the conversation and ask as Sholly was obviously in the middle of a story that might be derailed if he had to stop and supply background information. However, readers still might want to know who she is. Also, after reading a bit about her, I thought she deserved a few sentences of backstory. Footnotes are good for essays, but—although there is no rule against it that I am aware of—might seem awkward in an interview. I use my space as a chance to supply that background information. Finally, supplying this information provides a slight break in Sholly's words and a little bit more of a sense of a conversation, which usually reads better than the extended monologues that can happen in interviews (we'll examine those situations and talk about how to handle them in a later part of the book).]

Yes, she does. She came out into the reception room. She said, "Hi. Stan is busy. I'm sorry you can't meet him. What can I do for you?" I had this little shitty comic book that I had drawn, and I thought. "Gee, I bet Stan will like this." As a kid you don't have a clue as to whether what you did is actually any good or not, or else you're in denial about the fact that it's just amateur work. That's a blessing because it allows you to keep going and not get discouraged. She said, "We can't take things from outside sources. Good for you. Keep working." She was very sweet, but I didn't get in the office. I had the feeling from reading Stan's letters page that there was the bullpen and Steve Ditko, Jack Kirby, and everybody else were all in there working together, talking, and it was this big group **[gang having fun]! [note: I thought the cohesiveness and tight-knittedness of *gang* conveyed more of the togetherness and camaraderie Sholly expressed than *group*. The tone and pace of Sholly's words sounded like he imagined them enjoying being together but also having fun.]** It wasn't like that really, but that's the way Stan made it sound. ~~I tried to go see him. Like I said I ended up working at the same place many years later, so it did come around.~~

(16:14) ~~Right.~~ Did you save that little comic book that you had made up?

Somewhere. **[,s]**Somewhere ~~I have it.~~ **[note: Using the comma rather than the period narrows the time, the pause, between Sholly speaking the first *somewhere* and the second *somewhere*. Admittedly, this is a thin distinction to make, but I explain it in case you were wondering.]** I think I have it. It's just awful, though.

What was it about? **[note: Delving into origins and beginnings can be insightful. I also figured his early childhood work was a subject Sholly might not talk about as much.]**

It was a superhero named Nerve Master. I guess I was the one with a lot of nerve [*laughs*]. The character could control your nervous system, so he could make you think that you heard things and saw things that you didn't. I tried. It was just a few pages. When you're a kid, in those days at least, you didn't know that comic artists drew the pages bigger. You just saw the printed page and assumed that you had to draw it that size. My stuff was drawn on eight and a half inch by eleven inch paper. Just tiny. You think, "How do they do this? This is really small." Then later on you find out that's not how they do it.

But I always loved *Fantastic Four*. Growing up that was one of my favorite comics, so getting to work on a couple of movie versions of it was great fun. Anytime you're drawing *Spider-Man*, *Superman*, or *The Fantastic Four*, ~~whatever, professionally,~~ you stop to think, "*Damn*. This is cool."

(17:52) What is it about the Fantastic Four? Why do you like them so much?

Because of Jack Kirby, really. You know when I read those now, sometimes the dialogue is kind of ridiculous. They don't hold up that well for me, but the artwork does. Kirby's creativity is on another level. It looked to me like Kirby always wanted to entertain himself, and he wanted to have a good time. He would always start an issue off with this really strong visual to get you interested and get you excited and get you into the story. He has a really good sense of "What would I want to see? What would I think is cool?" and that came across.

[note: I made a paragraph break here.] Then, there was that period when he was creating the Silver Surfer and Black Panther, **[and Inhumans]. [This was the mid to late 1960s,] [note: This is factual information, which I include to give readers a little context. I could also have revised the passage so that I said, "And Inhumans. This was the mid to late 1960s" and Sholly could have picked back up with his next comment, "Which was just amazing." That's probably how I'd set it up now because, as I have said, I feel more comfortable adding words to what I say than adding words to what the interviewee says.]** which was just amazing. And Thor. At that same time, the *Thor* comic book was introducing all these incredible, new characters and they were in outer space and all sorts of places. Jack was really on a roll, creatively. It was exciting because this was all brand-new stuff. Now, there's thousands of issues of all these books. There's so much history, but in those days it was all pretty new. Every time the new Marvel comics came out—especially during the heyday of Ditko and Kirby—it was ~~only so many, so everything that they did~~ was fresh and exciting.

(19:39) So how did you get involved with the film? **[note: Now I tried circling back to *The Fantastic Four* to see if Sholly remembered anything else. You may have noticed this in your own experiences, but sometimes in the act of telling a story, more memories come back to us.]**

I don't remember who referred me, but a lot of storyboard jobs get referred. You work on a movie and **[maybe]** somebody there ~~maybe~~ likes what you did, so they get another movie and they say, "Hey, I met a guy that was a good storyboard guy. If you're looking for a guy, here's his information." The phone would ring and they'd say, "We're looking for a storyboard artist. Are you interested?" You say, "yes," and they send you a script, usually. You read the script and you're supposed to tell them if you're interested or not.

I got one script that I thought was awful. I thought, "Jeez, what am I gonna say about this?" The producer called me up and asked, "Did you get the script?" I said, "Yeah." She said, "Well, what'd you think? People either love or they hate it. Which were *you*?" I said, "I hated it, actually." She said, "Does that mean you don't want to work on it?" I said, "*No*, it doesn't mean I don't want to work on it. I'll do my best to do what I'm supposed to do, but you asked." They hired me and I worked on it, so they didn't hold it against me because I was honest. [**note: I broke this off from the previous paragraph and made this anecdote into its own paragraph.**]

What film was that?

Heathers. Winona Ryder. Christian Slater. The movie was actually a lot better than I thought it would be from reading the script. The script just didn't appeal to me for some reason. I read the script for the first *Buffy the Vampire Slayer* movie, and I did not get that job, but the script was great.

[**note: I could have cut those two paragraphs about Sholly's experience with *Heathers*. If this was something he had already talked about multiple times in other interviews, I would have. I thought people interested in Sholly and movies, in general, might want to read this. I also found his honesty refreshing and his initial take on the film struck me as humorous.**]

To answer your question, it was usually word of mouth and referrals [**that got me**] ~~where~~ jobs ~~would come from~~. I liked the *Evil Dead* movies, and I read in *Fangoria* or some place that Sam Raimi was making *Darkman*, and I thought, "Man, I'd like to work on that," so I called Tony Gardner, the effects guy. I had known him and worked with him. He was working on *DarkMan* and he told me to call Universal and ask for Sam Raimi. I called and they just put me through! I told his secretary I wanted to work on the film, she arranged a meeting, and I got hired. Sometimes you can aggressively go after something like that. Other times, you work for a director and they like what you did, so they hire you again. ~~Then, there's a connection.~~

(22:56) Did you ever meet Roger Corman?

Only once, just to say hello. I think I had a meeting with him once. I don't even remember why. I think I was trying to pitch

him a project or something. He was nice. He was friendly. ~~Nothing happened.~~

[note: Unfortunately, Sholly had little direct contact with Corman and what contact he had was not memorable. On the one hand, I hated to take what was already a short answer and trim it down since Corman is such an important topic in this project. On the other hand, "once" is redundant as Sholly said "only once" in the sentence right before. "Or something" is non-specific. "Nothing happened" isn't really needed. We can tell nothing happened and there really isn't a reason to include "nothing happened" since, well, nothing happened. I could probably have cut the whole question and answer since there is little information and it matches the standard account of those who have had brief contact with Corman. However, if I didn't include it, readers might wonder why I didn't ask Sholly if he had ever met Corman.]

~~(23:27) Do you have anything else that comes to mind?~~
~~(23:38) I wish I could tell you more about that specific movie.~~

[note: I cut this for similar reasons. If there is nothing to say, there's no need to say that there's nothing to say. Also, Sholly makes this same remark earlier about not remembering very much about the movie.]

~~I would say one thing about storyboarding for people who don't know what it is.~~ You start with a script, and you end up with a movie. Somewhere right in the middle is the storyboard. The storyboard is the point where the script becomes visible. You get the director's vision down on paper, and then everybody knows what he **[the director]** wants. The storyboard artist can have a lot of creative input and a lot of influence on things, or very little depending on the director's receptivity. [note: This segment appears near the end of the actual interview. I thought I would create a place for it at the beginning since Sholly's explanation works really well as an introduction and provides essential background information—what storyboarding is—and context.]

~~Discussion about what I was doing with this and the history of the project.~~ [note: The majority of interviewees asked me either at the beginning or end of the interview why I was doing this project and other associated questions. I explain this in the preface of *Forsaken,* so there's no need to include those instances in each interview that they occur.]

(26:15) [note: The following remarks come late in the interview. I added them to the second paragraph of the second response from Sholly as you will see in the final version.] I brought in Kirby comics and Kirby artwork to ~~Oley Sassone.~~ [him]. He liked it. I think he knew he didn't have the [an unlimited] budget and could only get so much on the screen. ~~I do have the sense that~~ [, but he liked and respected the material]. ~~That's just my impression of what he was like.~~ He wanted to honor the comics and what was good about the comics the best he could with the budget and so forth.

I spoke with him, and that's the impression that I had gotten that he really wanted to try to be faithful to the comics. It's one of the things I've heard, too, from a lot of people that the unreleased version is the one that's more faithful to the comic books, and I would agree with that.

[note: At this point, I took the remaining portion that follows and used that to close out the interview. At several previous points—around the 23:28 and 26:15 marks—the interview felt like it was possibly over. I could have turned off the recorder but I kept it running. As I advised earlier, keep the recorder on until you are absolutely sure the interview is concluded. I have sometimes waited until I either hung up or I heard the click of the phone hanging up on the other end.]

(27:31) I worked at Disney Imagineering for a few years also, for eight years, and I did a lot of stuff for them involving the Marvel characters for theme parks and things like that. That was another case of getting to draw Spider-Man, Captain America, Iron Man, and everybody. ~~All~~ [as] ideas for park attractions, things that you could do and play in parks ~~now that they have Marvel.~~ There was going to be a Doctor Strange ride and stuff like that. It was so much fun to storyboard Doctor Strange and what the ride would be like. That was another ~~thing where~~ [time when] I ~~can't~~ [couldn't] believe ~~I'm~~ [I was] getting paid to draw Doctor Strange and these characters ~~that~~ I grew up with *[laughs].* I don't think most of those things got made. You develop things and illustrate them and go through the process. Some things come out the other end and some things don't. I don't know what become of any of that stuff. It's all kind of secret. They wanted to do theme park things for Marvel. ~~Getting to draw those characters~~ [It] [note: I think I was trying to be concise. Looking back at it now, I would have left that original phrase in place.] was such a treat for a guy like me.

~~(28:53) I know there's the Incredible Hulk one and we went on it a few years ago. Do you recall if you did any of the stuff for that ride?~~

~~I did stuff involving the Hulk, but it's hard to say what happened to it. If it got used or not.~~

~~But it might have?~~

~~It might have.~~

[note: I was just kind of taking a shot with these questions about the Hulk ride to see if Sholly remembered anything else on the topic. It's clear that he didn't, and I didn't think those passages would have added much value to the interview, so I excised them. I asked primarily because since I had ridden the ride, I had a little bit of a connection to it. We were near the end, so I let the fan come out just a little bit.]

It's always fun to talk to people who love this kind of stuff because it's been a real ~~treat of a job and a~~ [fantastic] [note: I am not sure why I made this change, and I realize now I made an unintentional, but possible, pun with the word *fantastic*. Maybe I was concerned about the word *treat* coming up too often. Now, I would leave it as is.] career to be involved in moviemaking, particularly when they're good [movies.], ~~which they're not always~~ [note: I'm not sure why I cut this. Now, I think I might leave this in.]

~~Thank you, so much.~~ [note: I might include this in a single interview. In a collection, I cut this because I don't want to have one interview after the other ending in the same or a similar way. If I am writing for a specific publication, I look at how their interviews tend to end and model that. Sometimes they include greetings and goodbyes and/or small talk, and sometimes they eschew that.]

~~Discussion of sending him a transcription, timelines, and so forth.~~ [note: This is just summary of standard stuff nobody is interested in reading. I make a summary note to myself on the off chance that I need to go back to this at some point.]

so it was really fun to do the movie and draw those characters and stuff, [note: This is something that appeared much earlier. I move it to the end and edit it in the final draft.]

[It was really fun to do *The Fantastic Four* and draw those characters professionally.]

Final Draft Example: Pete Von Sholly

In this instance, Sholly did not have any suggestions or revisions after I sent the draft to him. What follows is the final, clean draft that incorporates all of the changes of the previous draft.

Pete Von Sholly (Storyboard Artist)

Please begin with an explanation of what a storyboard is.

You start with a script, and you end up with a movie. Somewhere in the middle is the storyboard. The storyboard is the point where the script becomes visible. You get the director's vision down on paper, and then everybody knows what the director wants. The storyboard artist can have a lot of creative input and a lot of influence on things, or very little depending on the director's receptivity.

Please talk about your involvement and what you did with The Fantastic Four.

I did all the storyboards for the special effects, the stunts, and things like that. I didn't work one-on-one with the director. Different directors work different ways. Oley basically just trusted me with most of it, so I went with it. Sometimes they want your ideas and input; sometimes they want to tell you exactly what to do. He was pretty easy to work with that way.

I brought in Kirby comics and Kirby artwork to him. He liked it. He knew he didn't have an unlimited budget and could only get so much on the screen, but he liked and respected the material. He wanted to honor the comics and what was good about the comics as best he could.

How many storyboards did you make?

I have no idea exactly. Many pages worth. All the effects sequences where somebody would stretch or transform, flame on, and things like that.

What kind of feedback did you get?

They seemed pleased with what I did. There was not a lot of nitpicking. I felt that once we'd seen Ben Grimm turn into the Thing, seeing it again was kind of needlessly expensive. I knew the budget was tight, so I did one shot where you're looking at his shadow and the shadow transforms, which I thought was a way to show variety in how the transformation happens and to make it more interesting visually. Oley was fine with all that kind of stuff.

So for that scene, you show it in full once and then there were other ways to suggest or represent it a little less expensively.

Yeah. I just thought also it would be more visually interesting. They didn't have CG effects to play with very freely. What year was the movie?

They were shooting it at the very end of 1992. Post-production would have been 1993.

Right. That was when *Jurassic Park* came out. So CG was sort of new and expensive, so it wasn't an option for them, I don't think, except maybe the Human Torch. They might have had some crude CG available for the Torch.

What was the process for making the storyboards? Did you look at the screenplay and then adapt images from that or how did this work?

You go through the script and look for sequences and scenes that require storyboarding. Storyboards are useful for the production people because you can imagine a thing many different ways. Not everything is explained just because it says on a page that somebody walks into a room and fires a gun. Okay, well, how does that work?

You could shoot that a hundred different ways. Once there's a storyboard of it, then everybody involved can look at that and go, "Oh, okay. I see what the director wants. I see what we need to do." So that's kind of the purpose of it. A lot of times they don't have the time or the budget to storyboard the whole movie, and so I would say to directors, "Well, what are your priority sequences? Maybe pick the shots that absolutely need storyboarding and make that your A-list. If we finish that and have time, do you have a B-list?" Some directors don't use much storyboarding, some don't use it at all, and some like to use it a lot. It depends on how much time and budget there is as to whether a film can have somebody like me on staff.

When you make that storyboard, that common visual reference for everyone, is that what everybody including the special effects team and the director refers to?

Yeah. I storyboarded a lot of movies in those years and in the 1980s a lot of *A Nightmare on Elm Street* movies, *Darkman* for Sam

Raimi, and stuff like that. Once the storyboards are drawn, everybody starts referring to them. Storyboards can even help with designing the sets. If you're storyboarding a scene that takes place in a room but the camera is only looking in one direction, maybe you don't need to build the whole room, or maybe you don't need to dress the whole room. If Reed needs to stretch, then what, exactly, does he have to do? Does he have to reach out to pick something up? Is it just him stretching? What is required? A storyboard lets everybody down the line know what their responsibilities are. Things change a lot from the storyboard stage. Sometimes things come out just like you storyboarded them, and sometimes they come out really, really different for a variety of reasons.

Are there examples of that that you can remember from The Fantastic Four?

No, I'm not that familiar with the finished film. Some directors like to sit with you and go through a sequence shot-by-shot and say, "Okay, I want to open with a wide shot, or a medium two-shot of these two people. Then I want a high wide angle of them. Then I want to boom down and push in on them." So you sort of figure it out beat-by-beat that way. Other times they turn you loose because they're busy or they want your input, so you get to kind of play director for a minute. In this case, I just remember having a lot of freedom and Oley liking what I did. I wish I had more specific memories and could tell you more. I know you're going to hear this a lot, but it was a long time ago.

I storyboarded a lot of films. You're interested just in this Roger Corman film, I assume?

Yes sir, primarily.

Okay. I ask because I worked on another version of it that didn't get made years later. Raja Gosnell was going to direct it. He directed the *Scooby-Doo* movie and some other things. This was another version of *The Fantastic Four* that we did a lot of work on, but it didn't happen for some reason.

So what happened with that version? This would have been after the unreleased Corman version but before the 2005 one that came out.

Yeah. It might have been Fox that was going to do it. I could tell that they didn't really understand the characters. They talked about the Thing like he was the Rock Guy, like he's actually made out of rock. I understand that you could look at him and think he kind of looks like that, but he's not made out of rocks. Jack Kirby actually told me once that the Thing is like a gorilla covered in dinosaur hide, so it's a scaly texture. It's organic. It's not rocks. In some of the concept designs people were putting crystals on the Thing and stuff like that trying to play with the idea that it was rocks. I was just shaking my head thinking, "That's not right" [*laughs*]. They were redesigning everything. It was just stupid stuff going on. I don't know why they ended up not making the movie, but I think it's just as well. They still haven't made a good *Fantastic Four* movie.

You actually met Jack Kirby, then?

A few times over the years. I was and am a big fan of Jack Kirby. To me that's the Fantastic Four.

Tell me about him. What was he like? What else did he tell you about the Fantastic Four?

Nothing about the Fantastic Four. He was a wonderful, polite, welcoming, gentle man. I went to his house a few times. His wife Roz would always welcome you and maybe give you a tuna fish sandwich and a cup of coffee or something. You were always treated like guests even if you were someone that had only met them at conventions and things. I bought a couple of pieces of original art from him over the years, so I went over and visited them. I was not what I would call a close friend of the family or anything like that. Roz usually handled the invitations and all of that. Jack was Jack sitting there doing comics. You'll never hear a bad thing about Jack from all the people who knew him, met him, and worked with him. He was always encouraging. What he always encouraged you to do was find you own style. Don't copy his style. Find your own style. Be yourself. He always had a good thing to say and was just the nicest man you'd ever want to know.

Did you ever meet Stan Lee?

I did. I worked at Marvel Animation for a while. Stan had an office there. I grew up reading *Fantastic Four*, so Stan and Jack were important to me. I didn't know the ins and outs. You know it's controversial about who did what, the credit and compensation, and all that. I didn't know anything about that. I just knew that when I grew up, I wanted to be Stan Lee and Jack Kirby because I wanted to write and draw comics. For me, those guy were big inspirations for that kind of comic. You could go into Stan's office and say hello to him. He knew who I was and I would visit. I was doing paintings and he would critique them if I asked. He was very lively and friendly. He would jump around and strike poses. He would say, "Well, look, in this drawing here, you should do this or try that." He seemed like he appreciated the fact that there were people who knew who he, Kirby, Ditko, and all of the Marvel comics makers were. They were important to people. He was not aloof or unfriendly at all . . . to me, anyway. It was just a special thing, to meet both of those guys. I was like, "Wow! These are the guys I grew up with, and here they are." Your heroes are real human beings. You can meet them and talk to them. It's very cool.

You mentioned Steve Ditko. He passed away recently. Did you have any interaction with him?

No, I didn't. I called him up once. When I was a kid, I was in New York at my Grandma's house on Flushing, Long Island. She had a phonebook that I was looking at, and there's his name, Steve Ditko. I called him up and he answered. What are going to say? "First of all, I didn't think you'd answer the phone. Is it really you?" He goes, "Oh, yeah. Yeah." He was still doing *Spider-Man* at that time. I just said some stupid stuff like, "Gee, you're great. I love your work" [*laughs*]. He was very friendly. He didn't say, "Don't bother me." I didn't get an unfriendly vibe. He seemed to just take it in stride because his phone number is listed, so people are going to call him up. That was it. I just got the impression of him as a friendly guy.

Marvel had offices on Madison Avenue in those days in the 1960s. My older brother took me there one day. He said, "Let's go see if we can meet Stan Lee." We went up and Flo Steinberg—who was this wonderful lady—who was Stan's secretary for many years. You might have heard of her.

"Fabulous" Flo. She did a lot things at Marvel. Left Marvel, came back, and in between published Big Apple Comix. Her name doesn't come up in comics as much as some others, but she has a very interesting story in her own right.

Yes, she does. She came out into the reception room. She said, "Hi. Stan is busy. I'm sorry you can't meet him. What can I do for you?" I had this little shitty comic book that I had drawn, and I thought. "Gee, I bet Stan will like this." As a kid you don't have a clue as to whether what you did is actually any good or not, or else you're in denial about the fact that it's just amateur work. That's a blessing because it allows you to keep going and not get discouraged. She said, "We can't take things from outside sources. Good for you. Keep working." She was very sweet, but I didn't get in the office. I had the feeling from reading Stan's letters page that there was the bullpen and Steve Ditko, Jack Kirby, and everybody else all in there working together, talking, and it was this big gang having fun! It wasn't like that really, but that's the way Stan made it sound.

Did you save that little comic book that you had made up?
Somewhere, somewhere I think I have it. It's just awful, though.
What was it about?
It was a superhero named Nerve Master. I guess I was the one with a lot of nerve [*laughs*]. The character could control your nervous system, so he could make you think that you heard things and saw things that you didn't. I tried. It was just a few pages. When you're a kid, in those days at least, you didn't know that comic artists drew the pages bigger. You just saw the printed page and assumed that you had to draw it that size. My stuff was drawn on eight and a half inch by eleven inch paper. Just tiny. You think, "How do they do this? This is really small." Then later on you find out that's not how they do it.

But I always loved *Fantastic Four*. Growing up that was one of my favorite comics, so getting to work on a couple of movie versions of it was great fun. Anytime you're drawing *Spider-Man*, *Superman*, or *The Fantastic Four* professionally, you stop to think, "*Damn*. This is cool."

What is it about the Fantastic Four? Why do you like them so much?
Because of Jack Kirby, really. You know when I read those now, sometimes the dialogue is kind of ridiculous. They don't hold up that well for me, but the artwork does. Kirby's creativity is on another level. It looked to me like Kirby always wanted to entertain himself, and he wanted to have a good time. He would always start an issue off with this really strong visual to get you interested and get you excited and get you into the story. He has a really good sense of "What would I want to see? What would I think is cool?" and that came across.

Then, there was that period when he was creating the Silver Surfer, Black Panther, and Inhumans. This was the mid to late 1960s, which was just amazing. And Thor. At that same time, the *Thor* comic book was introducing all these incredible, new characters and they were in outer space and all sorts of places. Jack was really on a roll, creatively. It was exciting because this was all brand-new stuff. Now, there's thousands of issues of all these books. There's so much history, but in those days it was all pretty new. Every time the new Marvel comics came out—especially during the heyday of Ditko and Kirby—it was fresh and exciting.

How did you get involved with the film?

I don't remember who referred me, but a lot of storyboard jobs get referred. You work on a movie and maybe somebody there likes what you did, so they get another movie and they say, "Hey, I met a guy that was a good storyboard guy. If you're looking for a guy, here's his information." The phone would ring and they'd say, "We're looking for a storyboard artist. Are you interested?" You say, "yes," and they send you a script, usually. You read the script and you're supposed to tell them if you're interested or not.

I got one script that I thought was awful. I thought, "Jeez, what am I gonna say about this?" The producer called me up and asked, "Did you get the script?" I said, "Yeah." She said, "Well, what'd you think? People either love it or they hate it. Which were *you*?" I said, "I hated it, actually." She said, "Does that mean you don't want to work on it?" I said, "*No*, it doesn't mean I don't want to work on it. I'll do my best to do what I'm supposed to do." They hired me and I worked on it, so they didn't hold it against me because I was honest.

What film was that?

Heathers. Winona Ryder. Christian Slater. The movie was actually a lot better than I thought it would be from reading the script. The script just didn't appeal to me for some reason. I read the script for the first *Buffy the Vampire Slayer* movie, and I did not get that job, but the script was great.

To answer your question, it was usually word of mouth and referrals that got me jobs. I liked the *Evil Dead* movies, and I read in *Fangoria* or some place that Sam Raimi was making something called *Darkman*, and I thought, "Man, I'd like to work on that," so I called Tony Gardner, the effects guy. I had known him and worked with him. He was working on *Darkman* and he told me to call Universal and ask for Sam Raimi. I called and they just put me through! I told his secretary I wanted to work on the film, she arranged a meeting, and I got hired. Sometimes you can aggressively go after something like that. Other times, you work for a director and they like what you did, so they hire you again.

Did you ever meet Roger Corman?

Only once, just to say hello. I think I had a meeting with him. I don't remember why. I think I was trying to pitch him a project. He was nice. He was friendly.

I understand you also worked with the Marvel characters for Disney.

I worked at Disney Imagineering for eight years, and I did a lot of stuff for them involving the Marvel characters for theme parks and things like that. That was another case of getting to draw Spider-Man, Captain America, Iron Man, and everybody as ideas for park attractions, things that you could do and play in parks. There was going to be a Doctor Strange ride and stuff like that. It was so much fun to storyboard Doctor Strange and what the ride would be like. That was another time when I couldn't believe I was getting paid to draw Doctor Strange and these characters I grew up with *[laughs]*. I don't think most of those things got made. You develop things and illustrate them and go through the process. Some things come out the other end and some things don't. I don't know what become of any of that stuff. It's all kind of secret. It was such a treat for a guy like me.

It's always fun to talk to people who love this kind of stuff because it's been a real fantastic career to be involved in making movies particularly when they're good movies.

It was really fun to do *The Fantastic Four* and draw those characters professionally.

*

While the first half of the Sholly interview, which focused just on *The Fantastic Four* would have been enough for the interview, I thought the Marvel information was unique and helped give insight into the film and the biographic information provided context. While I could have edited the collection down to just *The Fantastic Four* information and had a more focused collection, I felt this sort of secondary—but still relevant—information helps illuminate the film and is interesting on its own. Again, many of the people I talked with for *Forsaken* have not given that many interviews and I figured readers might investigate the book not just because of the subject but also because of a specific person they are a fan of. If we had gotten off on an irrelevant tangent about, say, favorite desserts, I would not have included that information.

If you have a strict word count you must adhere to, space limitations, or have been given a directive to focus just on a certain topic or topics, you should definitely edit down.

How to Handle Those Who Talk a Little or a Lot

A bad day, lack of time, introversion—for whatever reason, you may encounter people who talk in single sentences or maybe in even just a few words. I have not encountered that much, although I have had interviews move through the questions quicker than I anticipated. Of course, there is no law that says you must use all of your allotted time with an interviewee. However, if you only have half an hour or less, you will want to make the most of it. It's better to have some choice in editing out content than to be in the position of struggling to reach a certain length and not being able to edit down as finely as you might like. Sometimes interviews go quickly, interviewees burn through questions, you either need more material, or you want to maximize the time. For that reason, I would suggest having a B list of questions. These are questions you will only ask if you have exhausted your main list. I do not suggest making and keeping an all-purpose B list that you will use in each and every situation. Generic, general questions yield generic, general answers. Construct them specifically for the interview or project. There's nothing wrong with creating additional questions as you go, and in some ways that might be better because the actual conversation you are engaged in might generate specific, inspired questions. However, you don't want to *rely* on making additional questions in the moment just to have enough material.

More common are folks who will talk extensively. It might be their personality. It could be they are very passionate about the topic. Perhaps they are in a sharing mood. Maybe you just happen to be the right person who asked the right question on the right day. For whatever reason, they are going to *go*. If this happens, you are going to realize it very quickly. Treasure these people. Usually, they will make your job very easy. Just point them in a conversational direction and turn them loose. They will give you all sorts of great material, wonderful details, and answer questions you never asked but wished you would have once you hear them talk. Don't worry if you don't hit every question on your list. You might consider narrowing your list of questions down to just three to five of the most important questions if you think you will not get many opportunities to introduce questions and direct the flow of conversation. If there is something you absolutely must ask or you need to redirect them because they are going too far off topic for too long, you can always find an appropriate place to interrupt them and ask that question. From time to time, they may run out of steam and need a question to restart them. Yes, you will have more work when it comes time to move all those words from the tape to the page. However, that's like complaining your wallet is so full of money that it's hard to fold and sits heavily in your pocket. These are good problems to have.

Editing Talkers

Craig J. Nevius wrote the script for *The Fantastic Four*. He declined to be a part of the *Doomed* documentary about the movie. However, after the documentary's release, he decided he did want to talk (in fact, our interview begins with that very point). Nevius and I talked over three hours and the rough draft of our interview is slightly over forty-one double-spaced pages. Even in the context of a book of interviews, that's a pretty long interview. For the final versions, I trimmed about nine pages off, collectively. *Versions*. Nevius was there from the start, he had a lot of thoughts after filming was completed, and his post-Fantastic Four story was interesting. Splitting the interview into two interviews, with one tracking the origins of the film and the other discussing what happened after filming was completed, helped me to organize the content and break up the thirty-two pages (each interview was sixteen pages). I'll share my first pass of the first question of the interview.

*

You didn't participate in the Doomed documentary. Why?
I did not participate in the documentary for several reasons. I didn't want to revisit it all to tell you the truth. I literally just saw it a couple of weeks ago. After seeing it, I was so impressed by the eloquence and passion of the cast, Oley, and Glenn. I've been telling the story for years, which is one of the reasons I didn't want to tell it again. I was also aware that some people may have blamed Roger and/or Stan Lee when I'm not quite sure that that was entirely accurate. I wasn't sure how Roger and Stan Lee would be depicted. I enjoyed a good relationship with both men, worked with them both after *The Fantastic Four*. There were a couple of harsh comments about Roger. I don't think that they were inaccurate. I don't think he liked them very much from what I hear. I've not spoken to him about it. From what Mark related, he wasn't very happy with how he was depicted. I thought he was depicted accurately. After seeing the documentary, I was particularly impressed with Joseph, Alex, Oley, and Mark. They had a dramatic way of putting things that was very effective. I contacted Joseph afterwards.

At that point in my career, I was not a producer. I associate-produced a movie, *Stepmonster*, right before that, but I was not a producer on *The Fantastic Four* because there were so many to begin with. I was not a full producer at that time, anyway. As a writer, I was a bit more isolated from the group experience. I was there. Not every day.

I really had no idea that the cast felt as I did all these years. They still feel that way apparently. I thought Joseph spoke wonderfully and I thought Alex spoke emotionally. I was surprised and gratified that they all told our story so well and accurately. It's as fresh to them as it is to me. That was also a surprise to me. Had I known that before, I may have participated in the documentary. I don't regret not participating because I was credited in various ways and that was fine. I thought they were all great and completely accurate. That was gratifying to see the documentary, to hear everybody speak. I certainly think that there's a story here worth telling again as a collective. Over the years I've definitely beaten that drum, probably too many times. I know the others have occasionally but individually. As a group we sound like less like conspiracy nuts because we're all telling the same story, basically.

Alex maybe thought Stan was in on it. Alex seemed a little angry with Stan Lee. I get what his perception is. I didn't know about Stan Lee's comments at the time. That was complete news to me. This is not a put-down, and I don't think he would disagree: Stan is a showman in the best sense of the word. He is a storyteller and he can speak in sound bites, in boxes and bubbles. He may have been spinning it at the time. We only had one conversation about *The Fantastic Four* because I worked with him on a wonderful project in subsequent years which unfortunately did not sell, although maybe it would have a better chance now.

*

What you will notice is that although, there are some redundancies, there is some great content in Nevius' almost six-hundred word answer. However, you will also notice that a lot of his answer, although triggered by my question, is not directly related to my question. Fortunately, his answer relates to *The Fantastic Four* and he brings up people essential to the Fantastic Four comic and movie, whether Stan Lee, various actors, or other people who worked on the film. Because it is such a long interview, I took it through two more drafts before splitting it up. Once I divided it into two interviews, those each went through another draft before I came up with the final version for each one. What I'm going to show you now is how I took that first question/answer and broke it up to create multiple questions, plus a few tweaks. The version you will see is the final version, but I'll use strikethroughs to show what I eliminated.

*

You didn't participate in the Doomed documentary. Why?
I did not participate in the documentary for several reasons. I didn't to revisit it all, to tell you the truth. I literally just saw *Doomed* a couple of weeks ago. ~~After seeing it~~ I was so impressed by the eloquence and passion of the cast, Oley, and Glenn. ~~I've been telling the story for years, which is one of the reasons I didn't want to tell it again.~~ I was also aware that some people may have blamed Roger and/or Stan Lee when I'm not quite sure that was entirely accurate. I wasn't sure how Roger and Stan Lee would be depicted. I enjoyed a good relationship with both men, worked with them both after *The Fantastic Four*. There were a couple of harsh comments about Roger. I don't think that they were inaccurate. I don't think he liked those comments very much from what I hear. I've not spoken to him about it. ~~From what Mark related, he wasn't very happy with how he was depicted.~~ I thought he was depicted accurately.

~~I associate-produced a movie, *Stepmonster*, right before that, but~~ I was not a producer on *The Fantastic Four* because there were so many producers to begin with. I was not a full producer at that time. As a writer, I was a bit more isolated from the group experience. I was there but not every day.

I really had no idea that the cast felt as I did all these years. ~~They still feel that way apparently.~~ I thought Joseph spoke wonderfully and I thought Alex spoke emotionally. I was surprised and gratified that they all told our story so well and accurately. It's as fresh to them as it is to me. That was also a surprise to me. Had I known that before, I may have participated in the documentary. ~~I don't regret not participating because I was credited in various ways and that was fine. I thought they were all great and completely accurate.~~ That was gratifying to see the documentary, to hear everybody speak. I certainly think that there's a story here worth telling again as a collective. ~~Over the years I've definitely beaten that drum, probably too many times. I know the others have occasionally but individually.~~ As a group we sound like less like conspiracy nuts because we're all telling the same story, basically.

[*Alex seems to have some issues with Stan.*] [note: I create this comment, so that it breaks up the lengthy answer. Now, my inserted comment anticipates Nevius' next paragraph, which now responds to that inserted comment.]

Alex maybe thought Stan was in on it. Alex seemed a little angry with Stan Lee. I get what his perception is. I didn't know about Stan Lee's comments at the time. That was complete news to me. ~~This is not a put-down, and I don't think he would disagree: Stan is a showman in the best sense of the word. He is a storyteller and he can speak in sound bites, in boxes, and bubbles.~~ Stan and I only had one conversation about *The Fantastic Four* because I worked with him on a wonderful project in subsequent years which unfortunately did not sell, although maybe it would have a better chance now.

*

This next example includes a segment from an interview with Rebecca Staab who played the Invisible Girl / Sue Storm. We spoke for almost three hours. This interview went through a few drafts, including one in which Staab made slight changes here and there. What we'll look at one continuous answer that she gave me in response to my question about memories. I created and inserted several other questions to break up that answer and better match some of the paragraphs generated by the original question (as usual, I'll indicate my additions with bolded brackets and eliminations with strikethroughs).

*

What memories stand out about making The Fantastic Four?

It was really kind of twofold. It was the best of times; it was the worst of times [*laughs*]. We were playing comic book heroes. Does it get any more fun than that? We got to play, literally, PLAY, which is the dream of any actor. The people involved made it such a lovely place to be every day. Oley is one of the most incredible human beings on the planet. I just love him and how he embraced this. To him it wasn't just a job. It wasn't just a movie. It wasn't just directing. It wasn't just the shots. He was into the spirit of it and the authenticity of it. He really wanted to capture the feelings and the sentiment. All of us wanted to be true to the story for the comic book fans. There weren't really comic book movies before this. There was *Batman*, but this really predated this whole rush on all of these superhero movies. It was one of the very first ones. So to us, yes, were making a movie, but we were making a live-action comic book ~~that made it really interesting and made us feel very passionate because it wasn't just "Oh what scenes are we doing today?"~~ There was a constant awareness and a constant adjustment to either story or situation so that it would be accurate because we know how loyal comic book fans are and wanted it to be something that they accepted and they embraced. ~~That was our audience. It wasn't just general America or the general world. It was comic book fans and we knew that they knew their material, so we really had to rise to the occasion to really give them what they expected.~~ That dominant feeling through all of production is what made it different than any other film that I'd worked on. We had a goal that was bigger than just making a movie.

Everybody was on board. That was the great thing. ~~You can tell from the people that you've already interviewed. Everybody was extremely committed and enthusiastic and passionate.~~ Mark Sikes did a brilliant job with casting actors who were so committed and such great people. There was no ego or attitude. We were there as a team and working together whether it was on the days that we were shooting or when we weren't shooting. To this day, twenty-five years later, we're all friends. There's really nothing else that I've worked on that I can say that about. We're so lucky that that stage was set and it still has an energy and a life.

[*What about the budget?*] [note: I'm using the same technique I used in the example from Craig J. Nevius' interview. I create a question or comment that matches with the next answer to break up the answer and help pace the interview.]

What was also memorable was the almost miniscule and non-existent budget [*laughs*]. It was the epitome of low-budget. It wasn't just a low-budget film it was a super-ultra-low-budget film. We were aware of that and, of course, that affects everything. A lot of times it's frustrating. Time and money are the same thing. You don't have time for something because there isn't money for it and if you don't have money, there isn't time for it. ~~There's so much~~

~~more that we could have done and wanted to do that we just didn't have the luxury of doing because there wasn't a budget.~~ It was frustrating from a loving point of view because you always want to do more. You want to make this better, you want it to look like this—"let's do that again." When there isn't money, there isn't time and those things don't get done. That being said it's somewhat unites the team even more because you realize you're also up against that beast of budget and time. ~~It becomes even more of a team effort because~~ **[I]**~~i~~t's like, "~~Okay guys we have to do this and do it this way.~~ **,[t]**~~T~~his is all we have but we're going to have to make it our absolute best." ~~I think everybody rises to the occasion a little bit more when you're up against the wall and you really want it to be good.~~ We never threw our hands up and said, "It's low-budget. Who cares? ~~This is what it's going to be like." Instead it was "We don't have any money, but how can we still make it better?"~~

[*How were the conditions at the studio?*] [note: Again, I create and insert a question to break the original answer up. Notice how I don't come up with something random; I develop a question that makes it appear that the following answer is a direct reply to what I just asked.]

The conditions that we worked in were not great. I don't think I had worked on a show with that low of a budget. Even the studio that we were shooting in was actually condemned to be demolished. They told us that after we were finished shooting. Conditions in there were bad. Nobody had dressing rooms. We had one room all of us would hang out when we weren't on set. Our only luxury was we actually had a television in there. As far as catering, craft services, and coffee runs it was bare-bare-barebones.

It shows in the film. Whenever Sue was wearing everyday clothes, they were all my own clothes that I brought in. The only real "costumes" were our Fantastic Four suits and the wedding dress. ~~Everything else was my personal wardrobe.~~ When those conditions exist and you have that low of a budget, you better hope that you have a really good team and that's where we were blessed. We didn't have the money, but we had the team.

The sweetest thing is that it seems like every time an updated version of this film is made, our film gains more clout because people go, "You know what? At first I thought it was cheesy and low-budget but, whatever, it actually had a good storyline. It had a lot of heart as well. If it wasn't for the special effects this is probably the best version."

*

I took a 946-word answer from Staab and turned it into three edited answers of 354, 174, and 233 words (185 words were cut).

Robert Englund gave me an unbelievable amount of superior content in just over an hour. Here is the beginning of our interview.

*

Please talk about how you got the part of Ranger in Galaxy of Terror.

I don't know if you remember but back when we shot that movie, there was a big strike looming in Hollywood. Basically, for us, the actors, we knew that cable was coming. And we knew that a lot of our movies would be bought for cable. We were trying to negotiate so that we would get a nice residual payment. They were all telling us, "Oh, you bad actors, you're intimidating this infant industry, the cable industry." Now we all know the truth. We have a cable bill that's as long as our arm. What we were worried about is like you do a movie. In the old days, you'd do a movie. Sometimes they're a hit. Sometimes they're not. Sometimes they take a while to be discovered. But you always knew that movie was going to get picked up by one of the networks—CBS, NBC, or ABC—and it would be screened, *Friday Night at the Movies, Monday Night at the Movies*, or something like that. You'd get a primetime screening of your movie and millions of people in America would see it, and you'd get that nice, fat residual.

Well, cable would be doing an end run around that. Your HBO or somebody could buy your movie that wasn't a hit, and then they'd run it every night for a month before or after *Rambo* or something, but you'd get this little, tiny check. You wouldn't get this big, primetime network residual that we'd already negotiated. Plus, they would saturate that movie. It would be on so much, the networks wouldn't want to buy it now because it'd been on HBO every night, 24/7 for six months or whatever in what they call high rotations, and you just wouldn't get to see it, that non-cable money. We were worried about this big strike, and we were told that if you did a movie or a TV show and you negotiated it and went to work *before* the strike started, you could do that. You could finish that job. You could do that movie.

And the Roger Corman movie, *Galaxy of Terror*, fit right in to my schedule.

Now, I can't remember whether I knew Roger or whether I auditioned. I think I just had to meet Roger at his offices in Brentwood. That's my hazy memory. I can't remember if I met the director or not, but I think I just had to go meet Roger.

I was already an established actor then. I'd done lot of movies, a lot of A-list movies. I'd starred with Henry Fonda and Jeff Bridges. I had Susan Sarandon as a leading lady already, and I'd worked with some of the big stars of the 1970s like Burt Reynolds and Jan-Michael Vincent and people like that. People knew who I was in Hollywood. I think I just had to go meet Roger. I think that was my first time encountering him. I met this elegant, handsome guy who looks like an actor or a senator. I think he played a senator in *The Godfather*.

That's what happened to me. I got the part and I showed up at the old. He had just bought a new studio in the rapidly-gentrifying beach community of Venice, California. I already lived near there. I think I was still living. I'm not sure. I might have moved up into town by then, but for several years I lived in Venice and in Ocean Park, which is between Santa Monica and Venice. They have that great bike path and I was surfing down there and then I would commute into Hollywood for the west side, so I knew that area really well. I think I was even able to practically walk to work when I did that movie because I think I was living in Venice in the old part with the canals that were now filled in with earth and stuff. He had this great, new studio. I think it was an old lumberyard with warehouses he'd converted into a movie studio right in the heart of Venice, literally a block from the beach. All around it were these great new little restaurants starting up, sushi bars and community kitchens and things like that. My memory of working was kind of a wonderful experience as I remember it. Eddie Albert, Jr. took a lot of us out to lunch at the brand-new Rose Café, which now is an institution in Venice, but back then it was sort of the new hip thing. I remember Eddie taking us out several times for lunch, which was really gracious of him. He was a really classy guy.

*

I took that one chunk of 780 words and turned it into several questions. By now, you probably have a sense of how I do the sentence-level editing, so for this last example I am going to just show you the final version of the interview that utilizes the section above.

*

Please talk about how you got the part of Ranger in Galaxy of Terror.

Back when we shot that movie, there was a big strike looming in Hollywood. Basically, for us, the actors, we knew that cable was coming, and we knew that a lot of our movies would be bought for cable. We were trying to negotiate so that we would get a nice residual payment.

[How would the strike have potentially impacted residuals?]

In the old days, you'd do a movie. Whether it was a hit or not, you always knew that movie was going to get picked up by one of the networks—CBS, NBC, or ABC—and it would be screened on *Friday Night at the Movies*, *Monday Night at the Movies*, or something like that. You'd get a primetime screening of your movie and millions of people in America would see it, and you'd get that nice, fat residual.

Well, cable would be doing an end run around that. Your HBO or somebody could buy your movie, and then they'd run it every night for a month, but you'd get this little, tiny check. You wouldn't get this big, primetime network residual that we'd already negotiated. Plus, they would saturate that movie. It would be on so much, the networks wouldn't want to buy it. We were worried about this big strike, and we were told that if you had a movie or a TV show and you negotiated it and went to work *before* the strike started, you could still do that movie or show. And the Roger Corman movie, *Galaxy of Terror*, fit right in to my schedule.

[What was the audition for Corman like?]

Now, I can't remember whether I knew Roger or whether I auditioned. I think I just had to meet Roger at his offices in Brentwood. That's my hazy memory. I can't remember if I met the director or not, but I think I just had to go meet Roger.

[At that point, how much acting experience did you have?]

I was already an established actor then. I'd done lot of movies, a lot of A list movies. I'd starred with Henry Fonda and Jeff Bridges. I had Susan Sarandon as a leading lady already, and I'd worked with some of the big stars of the 1970s like Burt Reynolds and Jan-Michael Vincent. People knew who I was in Hollywood.

[What were your first impressions of Roger Corman?]

I met this elegant, handsome guy who looks like an actor or a senator. I think he played a senator in *The Godfather.*

[That's right. He was Senator #2 in The Godfather: Part II.]

He had just bought a new studio in the rapidly-gentrifying beach community of Venice, California.

[What do you remember about the studio and Venice at that time?]

I remember it all smelled like new wood and old scenery. I think it was an old lumberyard with warehouses he'd converted into a movie studio right in the heart of Venice, literally a block from the beach. All around it were these great new little restaurants starting up, sushi bars and community kitchens and things like that. I was surfing down there. **[I close my eyes a little bit when I'm talking to you and I can see that whole studio and imagine riding my bike over in the morning.] [note: This came from a portion of the interview around the halfway point.]**

[note: You might remember that in the first version of that question, there was some information about Eddie Albert, Jr. I used that later on in the interview for a question I asked about Albert during a sequence of questions about Englund's other *Galaxy of Terror* cast members]. *Edward Albert played Cabren who ends up replacing the Master. What was he like?*

He was a really classy guy. Eddie Albert, Jr. took a lot of us out to lunch at the brand-new Rose Café, which now is an institution in Venice, but back then it was sort of the new hip thing. I remember Eddie taking us out several times for lunch, which was really gracious of him.

*

I talked with Robert Englund for an hour and two minutes and my first draft came to twenty-four pages, which was almost 9,000 words. The editor only wanted the material directly related to Roger Corman and New World Pictures. That came to slightly under 3,000 words. I made an additional interview of about 1,500 words about Robert Englund and *Star Wars* that came from a question I asked on a sudden whim at the end of the interview. I gave that to *Fantha*

Tracks, a Star Wars website. I still have another interview of Hollywood-related reflections that comes to about 3,000 words that I am still sitting on (the other 1,500 words is either redundant or composed of snippets too short to use).

There's nothing inherently wrong with short answers or long answers, or short paragraphs or longer paragraphs, or short sentences or long sentences, but variety is good. As I wrote in an earlier section, the best interviews read like conversations—albeit conversations in which the interviewee does the majority of the talking—in which both people are participating and responding to one another. Mixing in some shorter answers helps give the interview a conversational feel as opposed to a monologue or lecture.

Questions for Martin Kove

I'll take you through another interview I did, this time with Martin Kove for one of the New World Pictures volumes. Unlike the opportunity with Sholly, I had time to prepare, so I'll start with the list of questions I had and you can check that against what I actually asked:

1. What Roger Corman films were you in?
2. How did you come to work on *Capone*?
3. Is it coincidence that you and Sylvester Stallone were both in *Capone* and *Death Race 2000*?
4. Please talk some about the experience of working on *Capone*.
5. In the extras for *Death Race 2000*, Corman says that "The audition with Martin Kove really was wild." Please elaborate.
6. Please talk some about your experiences working on *Death Race 2000*.
7. Any specific memories of any of the other actors?
8. What is the theme or message of *Death Race 2000*?
9. When you were making *Death Race 2000*, how did you think it would end up doing commercially and critically?
10. Gene Siskel gave *Death Race 2000* one star out of four. Roger Ebert was even harsher and gave it zero stars, though his feelings softened in later years. Others feel it's the greatest B-movie of all time. How many stars would you give it?
11. You worked with Stallone again on *Rambo: First Blood Part II*. Did you and Stallone ever talk about those earlier Corman experiences?
12. Corman is very efficient with a budget. Can you recall some examples of that?
13. Did you have any interaction with Corman?
14. What did you learn from working with Corman?
15. What's the best thing about working on a Corman production? The worst?
16. Did you have the opportunity to appear in any other Corman films?

17. In 2001 you played the villain FireArm in the *Black Scorpion* TV series with Roger Corman as executive producer. How did that come about and what was it like working with him again?

18. Your role in *The Karate Kid* as John Kreese is the character many people associate with you. Are there any connections between that character and any of the ones you portrayed for Corman?

19. You started studying martial arts in the early 1980s and later earned a black belt in karate. What lessons can you apply from karate to filmmaking, Corman, acting, and/or Hollywood?

First Draft Example: Martin Kove

Here is the first draft of Kove's interview.

*

(45:44)
(:25) **What Roger Corman films were you in?**

Don't you know? [laughs]

Well, I *know*, but I just wanted to go ahead and get it in the interview.

I got you.

You were in *Capone* and *Death Race 2000*, correct?

Yeah, but the first one was with Sly Stallone and Ben Gazzara called *Capone* with Susan

Blakely. All that stuff was in the first year of Hollywood. My first year in Hollywood I did like three movies and eight TV shows. Two of the three were Corman's. The first one was *Capone* with Ben Gazzara that was directed by Steve Carver. Then I went off and did *Death Race 2000*.

Let me tell you some of these great stories.

I'll mention stories in each movie and then you can add it in. As I talk about each movie, stuff will come up for me.

Okay.

(2:04). Good. In the first movie I was playing this guy Peter Gusenberg. Pete Gusenberg in *Capone* died in the St. Valentine's Day Massacre. It was fun playing a real-life guy. I liked doing research and all that for these characters. I found a lot out about Pete Gusenberg. He was in the O'Banion Gang, the North Side Gang. A bunch of Polacks and Irishmen fighting against Al Capone. I wanted to have a really cool gun. There was a scene where I walk up after ten cars shoot the shit out of this café trying to kill Frank Nitti and Al Capone. It really happened in real life. Twelve cars went by with machine guns and Thompsons. I stop. I get out of my car. I wanted to have a really cool gun. Everybody else was using Thompsons. I went into Stembridge Guns, where you rent guns Stembridge Gun Rentals, and I made this character always using antique weapons to kill people. He was using things like World War I flare guns. This guy Pete Gusenberg always had weird shit that he wanted to use as a torpedo, which is what they called it in those days. It's another word for a hitman. I went in there and I went around with a shopping cart and I got all these great, great weapons. *Great* weapons. I wanted to have a .30 caliber machine gun draped over my arm off the tripod, and I rented that, put it in the thing, and all of a sudden Roger comes up and says, "What's this?" And I said, "Well, I wanted to make the guy, you know, . . ." cause the director went for it. Roger says, "Do you know what this will cost?" He says, "You can have *one*. You just have a Thompson machine gun." I said, "Yeah, but everybody else has got a Thompson." Roger says, "No." He calls over the director, and then he leaves me alone with the director. I say, "Steve, look, you gotta at least give me two Thompsons, one on each arm." I shoot the shit. I get out of my car. It's a total definitive scene, and Steve said, "I've got two cameras shooting out on the street, two cameras shooting into the café. If one of these guns jams, we're in trouble. If just one jams, and there's no bullets coming out of it. So you can have one Thompson, which is jam-proof, and you hold it steady, and that's how you're gonna get it." Bottom line: It was a great scene, and I only got one Thompson.

That other thing that happened in that show was the prop guy gave me a double-barrel shotgun, and it's draped over the open window of a car I'm about to use to shoot one of our enemies. I'm in the driver's seat. Steve comes out. The double-barrel shotgun is aimed at his throat, and he's giving me a direction. I don't know what I was thinking. I actually didn't think there were any shells in there. And I answer him and finish the direction, put him at ease that I'm gonna do what he told me to do. I drop the shotgun down across my lap. BOOM! BOOM! (5:42) It blew giant holes the size of basketballs with these blanks. It was pointblank against the inside door of the car. If they had gone off on his throat, he'd be dead. It would have blown half his throat off. It was *unbelievable*. Ever since then I check five times the guns I use.

So that was two stories. The third story I found out years later while doing another movie that pertained to Capone. It was another movie with C. Thomas Howell called *Baby Face Nelson*. C. Thomas Howell played Baby Face Nelson and I played John Dillinger. This is 1998. We're jumping ahead because it's related. There's a scene where we rob a bank in the 1998 version of *Baby Face Nelson*. I'm in an open convertible, and guys from a rival gang are chasing me. I'm standing up in the back of the convertible. I've got a mustache, blue suit, and I'm shooting shells out of the back of the convertible with the top down. I never saw who was chasing me because it was all on camera. [7:14] A year later the movie gets released. I watch the movie and all of a sudden, the guy chasing me is in a tan suit. I have a picture of me in a tan suit. I recognize the car and the whole deal. I said to myself, "This looks really familiar." I zoom in with my VHS remote, and there it is: Marty Kove chasing Marty Kove. He had taken footage from *Capone* where I many times was hanging out of an old Model T shooting at someone. It was me, and only I would know this because I zoomed in the remote to see myself hanging out of that car, shooting at Martin Kove twenty years later playing John Dillinger.

That's great! Classic.

Unbelievable. *Unbelievable.* I have both movies now so I can show it to people, but the thing was I said to myself, "I wonder if Roger did that to pay homage to me, literally as a joke, as a very inside joke that only I would catch, or did he do it because he had stock footage and he owned it and he used it . . ."

To save a buck.

Yeah, which, of course, was what he was always doing. It was incredible when I found that out. So that was jumping to 1998.

I think between *Death Race 2000*, which was February of 1975. That was when Sly and I were friends in New York. We had the same personal manager, an old guy named Kuno Sponholtz. Kuno Sponholtz used to get Sly jobs as an usher in the Baronet in different theaters and get me a job as Santa Claus in department stores, so that's the kind of personal manager he was. We knew each other for years. [9:30] We did these two movies back-to-back, *Capone* and *Death Race 2000*. It was a lot of fun. In February of 1975, he's sitting in the motorhome with this red script, so I say, "Sly, what have you got there?" He says, "Ah, it's just a boxing movie I'm trying to make, man. I'm hitting a lot of dead ends." I said, "Good luck with it." So that was February of 1975. He got the movie made. Needless to say, it was *Rocky*.

In 1976, he literally called me and I was doing a TV series called *Code R*. I was in my first month shooting, and it was my first series in Hollywood.

You had been on episodes of other shows, but this was the first one where you played a character that appeared in multiple episodes.

Right.

I couldn't go to the screening of his movie, and he was pissed off because I was a good friend, and I couldn't go to see his premiere. The bottom line is he doesn't talk to me for *years*. I didn't do anything for Roger in between. It comes *Rambo* time and he puts me in *Rambo* and all that. I don't think I did anything for Roger until all of a sudden, 1992 comes along. In 1992, I finished *Cagney & Lacey*. I finished all the *Karate Kid* movies. I did all that stuff. 1992 comes along. There's a movie called *Firehawk* shooting in the Philippines and his old friend from USC Cirio Santaigo is directing it. Now, Cirio Santaigo has got racehorses. Cirio Santiago couldn't care less about this movie called *Firehawk*, but it was a good script and I loved the character. The writer and I used to have to fight Cirio Santiago to do coverage because he would shoot masters all the time. The guy would shoot masters all the time just so that he could get out of the set and get back to Manila where his horses were running. It was a long, long journey. I finished the movie. Good cast. I loved it. I see Roger in Beverly Hills every once in a while. I'll say, "How you doing?" and all that. I never did another movie for him.

Come five years ago, I'm sitting in the Directors Guild and they're having a screening of *Inglourious Basterds*. I wanted *Django* because I want to work with Tarantino, but I want to do a Western with him. I go to the screening. Five-hundred of my peers at the Directors Guild. I go there with my girlfriend and there on the day is Brad Pitt, Michael Fassbender, Diane Kruger, and Quentin. I raised my hand to ask a question and Tarantino goes, "Marty Kove! Marty Kove, you're one of my favorite actors. I loved you. You starred in this movie, *Firehawk*. It's one of my favorite pictures." Well, *Firehawk* was ultimately a piece of *shit*. I loved the character, but the movie didn't get the legs it should have gotten, but the character was great. A moment later, Brad Pitt grabs the mic and says, "And we just watched *Karate Kid* with my six-year-old daughter, and you've still got it Mr. Kove. You were great. You're a legend in our house." So I feel like a million bucks. I go back into the backroom. My girlfriend is taking pictures with Brad Pitt. Michael Fassbender comes up to me and says, "I love you, man. I've been following your career forever." This is like five years ago. I said, "Oh, really? Great." This is before Michael Fassbender hits. Bottom line is I felt like a million bucks. I exchange numbers with Tarantino. My night is complete. I'm feeling great, put the top down on my Porsche, lit a cigar, threw a scarf on and a cap. It was freezing that night, but I didn't even feel it because I had Quentin's number. I was gonna call him the next day and say, "Let's have a cigar and talk about doing a Western." Well, I get home and I can't read his handwriting.

Ohhhhhh.

For six months I did every option any actor could do to find this guy's phone number, couldn't get the phone number, and then ultimately he made good on his promise three years later by inviting me to come play in *Once Upon a Time. . . in Hollywood*. I'm in the opening scene. And it's a Western.

That's the history of Roger, and I really had such a good time working with his movies. Never made a nickel. I made decent money on *Firehawk*. In those days, I would do movies where I fell in love with the role. If a script was fair, I was arrogant enough to say, "Hey, my performance will make this script better," [15:04] which of course it never did. Each one of those epics I enjoyed so much for whatever reason. I was in Hollywood all of a year and I did three movies and eight TV shows, and I had such a good time playing those characters. I just did. Real-life characters are the most exciting to play anyway. You could do all the research on Pete Gusenberg and he had a brother. They died in the St. Valentine's Day Massacre. They were the guys who leaned again the wall. When I died in the St. Valentine's Day Massacre in that scene, all the stunt guys just went down like dominoes. I spun around, flipped over the chair. I did everything I could to make it a Hamlet death because I did not want to just fall down like all the stunt guys did. I think that's why my knees hurt, my shoulders hurt. Everything is bad because back in those days you didn't have a lot of lines so you try to do great action sequences.

(16:36) **In the extras for *Death Race 2000*, Corman says that "The audition with Martin Kove really was wild." What can you tell us about the audition for *Death Race*?**

I'm amazed that he remembers. Did he really say that?

He did it. I've got it in quotes because I reviewed the extras last week. He doesn't say much after that, and then it cuts to that first shot of you leaning out of the race car waving and smiling to the crowd. So I'm curious what you remember.

I remember that audition very clearly. I went in there after reading the script. Remember, he's Nero the Hero, so I went in there with a character really in that mold. I played it all—walk, gestures, voice. I just thought that was the essence of the character. I felt this Nero the Hero was so over the top. He was so full of himself. It was only a month after, two months after I did the other movie for him, and I was really feeling good as an actor. When you feel good, you take a lot of chances. I just felt that it was instinctive that Nero the Hero somehow as so many situations in Rome when you see Laurence Olivier with Tony Curtis and they cut that scene in *Spartacus*. Corman said, "Just take it down a little bit." So I took the vocal pitch down so that the voice wasn't so high. He loved it. He gave me the part. It was great [*laughs*].

(19:06) **What do you think is the theme or message of *Death Race 2000*?**

That's an interesting question. [*pauses*] Such a violent movie. I think the message could

be that if we don't lasso our own humanity now, that ultimately things like *Rollerball* with Jimmy Caan and *Death Race 2000* could actually happen. It's like the rise and fall of the Roman Empire. If you don't arrest some of the lack of humanity, you'll end up with cars hitting babies and people getting points for doing it. It's just the way it is. I think *Death Race 2000* is very pertinent to *now*.

My character John Kreese in *The Karate Kid* feels that kids are babied nowadays. They're *soft*. They get trophies for just participating, and I have a scene like that in season two of *Cobra Kai*. Marty Kove feels that kids who aren't the A players deserve acknowledgement. I'm not sure they deserve the same trophies, participation trophies, as the kid who scored all the goals in soccer. I'm not sure about that, but as far as Nero the Hero goes and a lot of people out there, they think everybody should get a trophy for participating in *life*. I don't think so. You've gotta have a high level of integrity and honesty to get a trophy in life, I think, along with whatever your prowess is.

(21:13) So are you saying that Nero the Hero and John Kreese are dissimilar or similar in that respect?

They're dissimilar because Nero didn't do anything. What did Nero do? (21:27) He drove a car and he hit people. He had no real expertise. The no-mercy concept for John Kreese is based on his experience in Vietnam. He would go up to a Vietcong boy with his platoon to give the boy chocolate and the kid was laced with dynamite and BOOM. That proved that mercy is for the weak because if you're showing mercy so many of his good friends die. So he came back, created Cobra Kai and the concept of no mercy, to win—not to lose. Because when he was in Vietnam he was never allowed to win like so many of our soldiers. John Kreese was allowed to win in high school and college. He was allowed to win in tournaments, but he wasn't allowed to win as a soldier, which he vowed would never happen again, and certainly not in his dojo.

Do you see any connections between Kreese and Pete Gusenberg from *Capone*?

I don't think John Kreese likes to kill people. I think he would only kill people in Vietnam when it was necessary and they proved dangerous. I think Pete Gusenberg was just a paid gun. It's a business. As actors, we've all interviewed people in the mob and spent time with people who are in the underworld. They're just terrific guys and lots of fun, but they're violent. It's a business, and I think it was a business for Pete Gusenberg. It's a business to *win* for John Kreese, but it's also a higher . . . It's about a level of morality and conviction. He doesn't get rich in the dojo. In the end of season two of *Cobra Kai*, he takes over the dojo. It's not about that. He didn't take over the dojo so that he can put more money in his bank. He took over the dojo because Billy Zabka, Johnny Lawrence, violated the concept, the integrity of Cobra Kai and became somewhat soft.

So if you could actually compare, I don't think that Pete Gusenberg or any torpedo who goes *soft* can make a living at all. I don't think John Kreese is a killer, but he could be for survival. Pete Gusenberg or any hitman is a killer by choice.

Good distinction.

(24:26) What did you learn from working with Roger Corman?

Well, I learned about his economics. I remember going up there and chatting with him about *Firehawk* in 1991, 1992. I was sitting at his desk. He was on the phone when I arrived, and I was listening to the phone call. I could tell from the dialogue that it was about another movie that was going over budget. As soon as he got off the phone, he went and shut off the air conditioner because the movie in that location was over budget.

[laughs] Wow.

So he was gonna save money that afternoon with the air conditioner off because that other movie was over budget.

I hope the air conditioning isn't still off.

I thought it was classic. [25:25] I cracked up hysterically, but I didn't tell him why.

So many great people worked for this guy. Jonathan Demme, Francis Coppola. I've got the VHSs of all these movies. It was really a great playground for the young director. Nowadays, kids make movies with the iPhones and all that. In those days, you had a *crew*. In those days, he financed movies that weren't expensive, but I think you got a better education in those days as a would-be director. He would let actors direct. I just thought that for me, as an actor, it was a great training ground. I think that you learn what not to do. You want a better dressing room. You want a few of the things you get later on in your career. You don't even know that the dressing room is second rate because it just *is*.

When you turn on that set and you're doing the action and you're doing the shooting and the falling and all that, as a young actor or a young director, it's heaven. You're getting to create your own destiny and your own art form. A lot of people owe him a great deal of thanks.

When you worked with Stallone again on *Rambo: First Blood Part II*, did the two of you ever talk about those earlier experiences with Corman?

No, but I talked about the earlier experience when I went to do the new version of *Kung Fu, Kung Fu: The Legend Continues* with Robert Carradine in the early 1990s. I played the Shadow Assassin. I was Carradine's nemesis, and I was stronger than he was. I was in a black duster and would come up only for the premier episodes of the three years and create havoc in his life. [28:00] One day at nine in the morning on the set, which made it six in the morning in L.A., he and I decided to call Roger and tell him that we wanted to do a remake of *Death Race 2000*. We called him up on the phone and he couldn't believe it. Both of us were on the phone. David, bless his soul, has a bottle of Hires root beer, and Hires root beer is brown. He's got this bottle, and it's clear liquid, so he was drinking at nine in the morning, Toronto time. We called Roger. Roger laughed at us and said, "Oh, how are you guys," blah, blah, blah. "Alright, sure, we'll do it" and he hung up on us. We had such a good time conceiving all the fun we had working with him because he and Stallone had the lead in *Death Race 2000*. Then, David and I became good friends after that. It was fun reminiscing there. Sly and I didn't reminisce too much about . . . We reminisced about Kuno Sponholtz, and we reminisced about *The Lords of Discipline*, [Flatbush?] a movie he did. He tried to get Perry King out and get me in there. He and I spent a lot of time . . . because he and I lived next to each other in 1974 when we both got out there. We had a lot of good times. I see him every six months. We talk a lot about *The Expendables*. He asked me if I wanted to be in it and I said, "Yeah," and then he didn't write the last one, so we'll see what happens.

[30:00] **When you were making *Death Race 2000*, how did you think it would end up performing in the box office and what did you think people's opinion of it would be?**

In those days, I didn't know. I really didn't know because I wasn't repulsed by it. When I did *The Last House on the Left* a couple of years earlier, I never liked that movie. I never liked it. I thought it was too gruesome. I was asked to play Krug, the lead guy, the chainsaw beast who kills the girls and all this stuff. I bowed out and David Hesse was my good friend at the time. I dressed him up in a sweater and I brought him into that to meet Sean Cunningham and Wes Craven. It was Wes Craven's first movie, and David got the part, and he also wrote the music. But I never got a real negative feeling from *Death Race 2000* until I saw it in its entirety. Then I realized . . . I love babies so much. I have a two-year-old grandson and a four-year-old granddaughter. I could never conceive some of those things of the car hitting the babies, and there was a bomb in it. My character going after a baby carriage . . . Some of that to me was over the top, but it was far more entertaining as a whole movie. But you look at it as an actor, look at the actions of the individual character, and it's a little over the top. [31:34] Now you're doing other things like I did the Tarantino movie and *Cobra Kai* and it's a whole different world because you're more seasoned, and yet you've gotta go through the Roger Corman school of learning what's appropriate and what's not as a talent. You make mistakes, you rectify them, and he give you an arena to make the mistakes.

Is it okay if I ask you one more question?
Yeah. Go ahead.
[32:09] **We talked about how you studied martial arts and I read that you have a black belt in karate. What lessons or**

principles can you apply from karate to filmmaking, Corman, acting, and/or Hollywood?

Discipline.

Sheer discipline.

Karate is about discipline. Karate is about focus. Karate, according to Mr. Miyagi, was defined as a defensive art. John Kreese defines it as an offensive sport. There are some people that if they win in the tournament, it's enough. John Kreese's concept is it's not about just the tournament; it's about that your enemy, your opponent doesn't get up because on the street if you let someone get up, you endanger your life. He applies the same thing from the streets to a tournament.

[33:23] But in either case, acting or directing for Roger Corman or anyone, it's discipline. It's discipline to do your homework. It's discipline to do your backstories. Discipline to really have a couple of alternatives as an actor to play with. If something doesn't work out, you have a plan B, plan C. I think in the arena of making a movie, any movie, my son's doing a movie. He's got a great movie coming out called *D-Day*. His name is Jesse Cove, terrific little actor. He and Weston Cage, Nic's kid, try[?] leads in this movie *D-Day*, which is out September 13 in the theaters. It's a great story about two-hundred rangers destroying howitzers that were about to bomb Omaha Beach, about to destroy the ships coming in. He did a great job, and yet he just is off now doing a movie for nothing. I told him, "Jesse, this is the lead. It's a good script. Go do it." He said, "Dad, I don't want to work for nothing." I said, "Go do it. They'll take care of you. I've worked for the producer two other times, once in London as a pilot for a piece."

[34:50] I spoke to him today and he's having a great time. He didn't want to do it—no money. I think any arena where you like the material, where you like the role, whether it's Roger Corman or you're working for John Avildsen or you're working for Michael Bay or Quentin—that movie had more trucks on the set than trucks for fruit, trucks for ice cream, trucks for popcorn. I didn't get paid much money on that movie, but to work for Quentin, be in a movie with Quentin . . . You learn that early on when you're with Roger. You have the opportunity to exercise your craft, whether you're a director or a prop man or you're an actor starting out, you go for it. That's the discipline we have to use as young actors. I think young actors have to use it, and even I would use it now. [35:54]

If a project came along that I loved, and I was getting paid nine dollars, like a Western somewhere, I'd go do it because you only can benefit by it, man. You can only benefit by it. The through-line of all of this is discipline. When you have the opportunity to exercise your discipline, make it happen.

38:51 As bizarre as that movie was [DR 2000], it was so much fun to work for him.

So I did *Capone*, *Death Race 2000*, *Baby Face Nelson*, and *Firehawk*. Did I do anything in between?

There was also . . .

Oh, yeah. The series! I did the series! That's right. I did . . .

Black Scorpion.

Yeah, what the hell was the character's name?

Firearm.

Firearm. Right! I took my ten-year-old son on the set. He had a ball. I've got so many photographs of that show. The chick was fantastic. She went off, left her career after that. She left to do something with movies with a preacher up in Oregon. But she was great-looking. It was the first series I think he did. [39:55].

We kept going back and shooting more stuff. I had a great time. I really had a good time on that show. So many celebrities came and did pickup shots and we all bumped into each other. Yeah, that was . . . My kids were ten, so that must've been about 2000.

2001.

Yeah. That would have been the last thing I did for him, I think.

Did you ever have the opportunity to work on any of his other projects and you said no, the timing didn't work out, or otherwise declined, or were those the only offers you got from Corman?

[*long pause*] There might have been a couple of others. I can't remember. Those five are the ones I really remember stories from. I don't think so.

I remember the worst refusal I ever did, but it wasn't a Roger Corman movie. It was *Tom Horn* and I was going to play . . . You talk about big mistakes. I was offered to play Gentleman Jim Corbett, a week's work, with Steve McQueen in *Tom Horn*, the last Western he made. He was my idol. I'll never forget it. What a dumb thing. I arrived in New York to see my parents. The phone call came in that *day*. I didn't want to upset my parents and leave the next morning because I had to if I took the part, and I passed on it. Then he passed away about a year later. That was the *worst* decision I ever made in my life. The worst—as far as the career goes.

42:07 **The only thing I wanted to add is I know the main focus of this is supposed to be Roger Corman and his stuff with New World Pictures, but I really love *The Karate Kid* and your work in it. I saw it when it first came out in the theater when I was a kid. It resonated with me then, and it's stayed with me through my whole adult life. Just to be a fan for a second, I just wanted to tell you that and how much I enjoyed it.**

Well, thank you very much. That's very kind of you.

[note: This is when we started talking about the *Cobra Kai* series, then available only on *YouTube Red*, the predecessor to *YouTube Premium*. I admitted to him I had not seen the series but I didn't want to admit that in the interview. For the record, I have since seen every episode on *Netflix*, and it is great stuff.]

Cobra Kai, of course, picks up with a lot of that story and those characters.

Can we talk a little bit about that and your role?

Absolutely. I enter in episode ten, and I set up season two.

43:15 It's a great show. It's not white hats and black hats like the movie. My character is written with some vulnerability, lots of versatility. You'll end up binging it. You'll binge five episodes a night. It's thirty minutes long. It's brilliantly written. Ralph Macchio is in it and William Zabka who played Johnny Lawrence. He kind of starred in it. They're the two stars in it. I come in episode ten, season one, and I blow the whole thing wide open. We are the most streamed show on the planet. It doesn't matter what they are; they all come in second. The only show watched more than us was a network show called *Game of Thrones*. That's how good this show is. So just get it and watch it. You'll love it. They bring in flashbacks, and these cats are so smart. They went to the archives of Columbia, the three writers, and they got angles and cuts from scenes that were in the movie but they were different outtakes, so they were different angles. So when you're watching these episodes and you see flashbacks of the movie, it looks like you remember it, but they're different angles.

Oh, that's so cool.

That's the kind of research these guys did.

Why wait? Just order it now, and then cancel your subscription. You can watch twenty episodes of nothing but terrific writing and a lot of great memories for you. It's good stuff. It's *really*, really good.

Okay, my friend, take care of yourself. Call Steve and tell Steve if you had a good time. He always likes to hear about my activity.

Thanks so much. I'll give you a great report.

*

Second Draft Example Including Corrections, Edits, and Revisions: Martin Kove

Now, we'll look at a draft that transitions from first to final. Just like with the Pete Von Sholly interview, I will use the strikethrough line to indicate passages and words I cut. Insertions are in bolded brackets. Explanatory notes are bolded in brackets and begin with "note" and a colon.

*

What Roger Corman films were you in?

Don't you know? [laughs]

Well, I *know*, but I just wanted to go ahead and get it in the interview.

I got you.

You were in *Capone* and *Death Race 2000*, correct?

Yeah~~,~~ [.] ~~but the first one was with Sly Stallone and Ben Gazzara called *Capone* with Susan Blakely. All that stuff was in the first year of Hollywood.~~ My first year in Hollywood I did like three movies and eight TV shows. ~~Two of the three were Corman's.~~ The first one was *Capone* with Ben Gazzara [**, Sly Stallone, and Susan Blakely**]. [**T**]that was directed by Steve Carver. Then I went off and did *Death Race 2000*.

[Those were the two movies for New World Pictures.]

[Yes.] Let me tell you some of these great stories.

[Yes, please.]

~~I'll mention stories in each movie and then you can add it in. As I talk about each movie, stuff will come up for me.~~

~~**Okay.**~~

~~Good.~~ In [**Capone**] ~~the first movie~~ I was playing this guy[**, Peter Gusenberg,**]~~.~~ ~~Pete Gusenberg in *Capone*~~ [**who**] died in the St. Valentine's Day Massacre. It was fun playing a real-life guy. I liked doing research and all that for these characters. ~~I found a lot out about~~ Pete Gusenberg~~.~~ ~~He~~ was in the O'Banion Gang, the North Side Gang~~,~~ [**,**

which was a] A bunch of the Polish and Irishmen fighting against Al Capone.

I wanted to have a really cool gun. There was a scene where I walk up after ten cars **[have]** shoot **[shot]** the shit out of this café trying to kill Frank Nitti and Al Capone. It really **[,which]** happened in real life. Twelve cars went by with machine guns and Thompsons. I stop. I get out of my car. I wanted to have a really cool gun **[something different].** Everybody else was using Thompsons. **[note: Now, I would reverse the order of the previous two sentences.]** I went into Stembridge Guns, where you rent guns Stembridge Gun Rentals, and I made **[had the idea of] [note: I might use *created* instead of *had*.]** this character always using antique weapons to kill people. He was using things like World War I flare guns. This guy Pete Gusenberg always had weird shit that he wanted to use**[. He was]** as a torpedo, which is what they called it in those days. It's another word for a hitman. I went in there **[Stembridge,]** and I went around with a shopping cart and I got all these great, great weapons. *Great* weapons.

I wanted to have a .30 caliber machine gun **[removed from the tripod and]** draped over my arm**[.]** off the tripod, and I rented that, put it in the thing, and all of a sudden Roger comes up and says, "What's this?" And I said, "Well, I wanted to make the guy, you know, . . ." cause the director went for it. **["The director went for it" appears after the first sentence in this paragraph.]** Roger says, "Do you know what this will cost?" He says, "You can have *one*. You just have a Thompson machine gun." I said, "Yeah, but everybody else has got a Thompson." Roger says, "No." He calls over the director, and then he leaves me alone with the director. I say, "Steve, look, you gotta at least give me two Thompsons, one on each arm.[22] I shoot the shit. **I get out of my car. It's a total definitive scene[."]** **[note: I extended the quote, so that instead of Kove telling me that information, it's now Kove telling me what he told Carver, which I think sounds clearer.]** , and Steve said, "I've got two cameras shooting out on the street, two cameras shooting into the café. If one of these guns jams, we're in trouble. If just one jams, and there's no bullets coming out of it **[there's a problem].** So you can have one Thompson, which is jam-proof, and you hold it steady, and that's how you're gonna get it." Bottom line: It was a great scene, and I only got one Thompson.

That other thing that happened in ~~that show~~ [*Capone*] was [**that**] the prop guy gave me a double-barrel shotgun, and it's draped over the open window of a car I'm about to use to shoot one of our enemies. I'm in the driver's seat. Steve comes out [**to talk**]. The double-barrel shotgun is aimed at his throat, and he's giving me a direction. I don't know what I was thinking. I actually didn't think there were any shells in there. ~~And~~ I answer him and finish the direction, put him at ease that I'm gonna do what he told me to do. I drop the shotgun down across my lap. BOOM! BOOM! It blew giant holes the size of basketballs with these blanks. It was pointblank against the inside door of the car. If they had gone off on his throat, he'd be dead. It would have blown half his throat off. It was *unbelievable*. Ever since then I check ~~five times~~ the guns I use [**five times**].

So that was two stories. The third story I found out years later while doing another movie that pertained to Capone. ~~It was another movie with C. Thomas Howell called~~ [,] *Baby Face Nelson*. C. Thomas Howell played Baby Face Nelson and I played John Dillinger. This is ~~1998~~ [**1996**]. We're jumping ahead [**chronologically**] because it's related. There's a scene where we rob a bank in the ~~1998~~ [**1996**] version of *Baby Face Nelson*. I'm in an open convertible, and guys from a rival gang are chasing me. ~~I'm standing up in the back of the convertible.~~ I've got a mustache, blue suit, and I'm shooting shells out of the back of the convertible with the top down. I never saw who was chasing me [**because it was all on camera**].

A year later ~~the movie~~ [**Baby Face Nelson**] gets released. I watch the movie and all of a sudden, the guy chasing me is [**appears**] in a tan suit. I have a picture of me in a tan suit. I recognize the car and the whole deal. I said to myself, "This looks really familiar." I zoom in with my VHS remote, and there it is: Marty Kove chasing Marty Kove. ~~He~~ [**Corman**] had taken footage from *Capone* where ~~I~~ many times [**I**] was [**note: Moving "I" makes it less awkward, but it still sounds clunky. Now, I would probably make the same change but remove "many times" and add "repeatedly" in front of "hanging out," so that the passage would say "where I was repeatedly hanging out."**] hanging out of an old Model T shooting at someone. It was me, and only I would know this because I zoomed in [**with**] the remote to see myself hanging out of that car, shooting at Martin Kove twenty years later playing John Dillinger.

That's great! Classic.

Unbelievable. *Unbelievable*. I have both movies now so I can show it to people, ~~but the thing was~~ [.] I said to myself, "I wonder if Roger did that to pay homage to me, literally as a joke, as a very inside joke that only I would catch, or did he do it because he had the stock footage and he owned it and he used it . . ."

To save a buck.

Yeah, which, of course, was what he was always doing. It was incredible when I found that out. So that was jumping to ~~1998~~ **[1996]**.

~~I think between~~ **[Now I'm moving back to]** *Death Race 2000*, which was February of 1975. That was when ~~Sly~~ **[Sylvester Stallone]** and I were friends in New York. We had the same personal manager, an old guy named Kuno Sponholtz. Kuno Sponholtz used to get Sly jobs as an usher in the Baronet in different theaters and get me a job as Santa Claus in department stores, so that's the kind of personal manager he was. We knew each other for years. ~~We~~ **[Stallone and I]** did these two movies back-to-back, *Capone* and *Death Race 2000*. It was a lot of fun. In February of 1975, he's sitting in the motorhome with this red script, so I say, "Sly, what have you got there?" He says, "Ah, it's just a boxing movie I'm trying to make, man. I'm hitting a lot of dead ends." I said, "Good luck with it." So that was February of 1975. He got the movie made. Needless to say, it was *Rocky*.

In 1976, he literally called me and I was doing a TV series called *Code R*. I was in my first month shooting, and it was my first series in Hollywood.

You had been on episodes of other shows, but this was the first one where you played a character that appeared in multiple episodes.

Right.

I couldn't go to the screening of ~~his movie~~ **[Rocky]**, and he was pissed off because I was a good friend, and I couldn't go to see his premiere. The bottom line is he doesn't talk to me for *years*. I didn't do anything for Roger in between. It comes *Rambo* time and he puts me in *Rambo* **[: First Blood Part II]** ~~and all that~~.

[note: When you see the final draft, you'll notice that I move a lot of material around so that it doesn't jump from years, people, and movies quite so much. If I try to represent all of those changes here, I think it might be too confusing. Instead, I'll continue to show sentence level edits and you can compare the

actual movement of paragraphs between drafts by flipping between this draft and the final draft.]

[**After *Capone* and *Death Race 2000*,**] I don't think I did anything for Roger until ~~all of a sudden,~~ 1992 ~~comes along~~. In 1992, I finished *Cagney & Lacey*. I finished all the *Karate Kid* movies. ~~I did all that stuff. 1992 comes along~~. There's a movie called *Firehawk* shooting in the Philippines and ~~his~~ [**Roger's**] old friend ~~from USC~~ [**,**]Cirio Santaigo[**,**] is directing it. Now, Cirio Santaigo has got racehorses. Cirio Santiago couldn't care less about this movie called *Firehawk*, but it was a good script and I loved the character. The writer and I used to have to fight Cirio Santiago to do coverage because he would shoot masters all the time~~. The guy would shoot masters all the time~~ just so that he could get out of the set and get back to Manila where his horses were running. It was a long, long journey. I finished the movie. Good cast. I loved it.

I see Roger in Beverly Hills every once in a while. I'll say, "How you doing?" and all that. I never did another movie for him [**after *Baby Face Nelson***].

[**How did you come to *Once Upon a Time. . . in Hollywood*?**]

~~Come~~ [**F**]five years ago, I'm sitting in the Directors Guild and they're having a screening of *Inglourious Basterds*. I wanted *Django* [***Unchained***] because I want to work with Tarantino, but I want to do a Western with him. I go to the screening. Five-hundred of my peers [**are**] at the Directors Guild. I go there with my girlfriend and there on the day is Brad Pitt, Michael Fassbender, Diane Kruger, and Quentin. I raised my hand to ask a question and Tarantino goes, "Marty Kove! Marty Kove, you're one of my favorite actors. I loved you. You starred in this movie, *Firehawk*. It's one of my favorite pictures." Well, *Firehawk* was ultimately a piece of *shit*. I loved the character, but the movie didn't get the legs it should have gotten, but the character was great. A moment later, Brad Pitt grabs the mic and says, "And we just watched [***The***] *Karate Kid* with my six-year-old daughter, and you've still got it Mr. Kove. You were great. You're a legend in our house." So I feel like a million bucks. I go back into the backroom. My girlfriend is taking pictures with Brad Pitt. Michael Fassbender comes up to me and says, "I love you, man. I've been following your career forever." ~~This is like five years ago.~~ I said, "Oh, really? Great." This is before Michael Fassbender hits. ~~Bottom line is I felt like a million bucks.~~ [**note: I cut this as "felt like a million dollars" is a stock expression, and I think readers**

know how great Kove feels from his descriptive narration of the event].

I exchange numbers with Tarantino. My night is complete. I'm feeling great, put the top down on my Porsche, lit a cigar, threw a scarf on and a cap. It was freezing that night, but I didn't even feel it because I had Quentin's number. I was gonna call him the next day and say, "Let's have a cigar and talk about doing a Western." Well, I get home and I can't read his handwriting.

Ohhhhhh. [What a tough break.] [note: As I have pointed out before, some responses such as "yeah" can be difficult to interpret. I thought "Ohhhhhh" was another one of those, so I added "What a tough break."]

For six months I did every[**thing**] ~~option~~ any actor could do to find this guy's phone number, couldn't get the phone number, and then ultimately he made good on his promise three years later by inviting me to come play in *Once Upon a Time. . . in Hollywood*. I'm in the opening scene. And it's a Western.

That's the history of Roger, and I really had such a good time working with his movies.

[How was the pay?]

Never made a nickel. I made decent money on *Firehawk*. In those days, I would do movies where I fell in love with the role. If a script was fair, I was arrogant enough to say, "Hey, my performance will make this script better," which of course it never did. Each one of those epics I enjoyed so much for whatever reason.

~~I was in Hollywood all of a year and I did three movies and eight TV shows, and I had such a good time playing those characters. I just did. Real-life characters are the most exciting to play anyway. You could do all the research on Pete Gusenberg and he had a brother. They died in the St. Valentine's Day Massacre. They were the guys who leaned again the wall.~~

[Please talk about Pete Gusenberg's death in *Capone*.]

When I died in the St. Valentine's Day Massacre ~~in that scene,~~ all the stunt guys just went down like dominoes **[in that scene]**. I spun around, flipped over the chair. I did everything I could to make it a Hamlet death because I did not want to just fall down like all the stunt guys did. I think that's why my knees hurt, my shoulders hurt. Everything **[on my body]** is bad because back in those days you didn't have a lot of lines so you**['d]** try to do great action sequences.

In the extras for *Death Race 2000*, Corman says that "The audition with Martin Kove really was wild." What can you tell us about the audition for *Death Race*?

I'm amazed that he remembers [**that audition**]. Did he really say that?

He did it. I've got it in quotes because I reviewed the extras last week. ~~He doesn't say much after that, and then it cuts to that first shot of you leaning out of the race car waving and smiling to the crowd.~~ **So I'm curious what you remember.**

I remember that audition very clearly. I went in there after reading the script. Remember, he's Nero the Hero, so I went in there with a character really in that [**Roman**] mold. I played it all—walk, gestures, voice. I just thought that was the essence of the character. I felt this Nero the Hero was so over the top. He was so full of himself. It was only a month after, two months after I did ~~the other movie~~ [**Capone**] for ~~him~~ [**Corman**], and I was really feeling good as an actor. When you feel good, you take a lot of chances. ~~I just felt that it was instinctive that Nero the Hero somehow as so many situations in Rome when you see~~ [**I thought about**] Laurence Olivier with Tony Curtis ~~and they cut that scene~~ in *Spartacus*. Corman said, "Just take it down a little bit." So I took the vocal pitch down so that the voice wasn't so high. He loved it. He gave me the part. It was great [*laughs*].

What do you think is the theme or message of *Death Race 2000*?

That's an interesting question. [*pauses*] Such a violent movie. I think the message could

be that if we don't lasso our own humanity now, that ultimately things like *Rollerball* with Jimmy Caan and *Death Race 2000* could actually happen. It's like the rise and fall of the Roman Empire. If you don't arrest some of the lack of humanity, you'll end up with cars hitting babies and people getting points for doing it. It's just the way it is. I think *Death Race 2000* is very pertinent to *now*.

My character John Kreese in *The Karate Kid* feels that kids are babied nowadays. They're *soft*. They get trophies for just participating, and I have a scene like that in season two of *Cobra Kai*. Marty Kove feels that kids who aren't the A players deserve acknowledgement. I'm not sure they deserve the same trophies, participation trophies, as the kid who scored all the goals in soccer. I'm not sure about that, but as far as Nero the Hero goes and a lot of people out there, they think everybody should get a trophy for participating in *life*. I don't think so. You've gotta have a high level of integrity and honesty to get a trophy in life, I think, along with whatever your prowess is.

So are you [are] saying that Nero the Hero and John Kreese are dissimilar or similar in that respect[, right]?

They're dissimilar because Nero didn't do anything.

[The title of "Hero" for Nero is kind of ironic, then, and unearned in your estimation.]

What did Nero do? He drove a car and he hit people. He had no real expertise.

[I'm thinking, too, about how they're both earning or focused on earning points in their movie's respective sports. Nero's method is driving over innocent pedestrians who are mostly unwilling and unarmed. John Kreese's method—at least within the tournaments—involves willing participants who are more or less equally matched and fighting hand-to-hand, not body-to-car. At the same time, it seems that neither believes in showing mercy.]

The no-mercy concept for John Kreese is based on his experience in Vietnam. He would go up to a Vietcong boy with his platoon to give the boy chocolate and the kid was laced with dynamite and BOOM. That proved that mercy is for the weak because if you're [by] showing mercy so many of his good friends die[d]. So he came back, created Cobra Kai and the concept of no mercy, to win—not to lose. Because when he was in Vietnam he was never allowed to win like so many of our soldiers **[were not allowed to win]**. John Kreese was allowed to win in high school and college. He was allowed to win in tournaments, but he wasn't allowed to win as a soldier, which he vowed would never happen again, and certainly not in his dojo.

Do you see any connections between Kreese and Pete Gusenberg from *Capone*?

I don't think John Kreese likes to kill people. I think he would only kill people in Vietnam when it was necessary and they proved dangerous. I think Pete Gusenberg was just a paid gun. It's a business. As actors, we've all interviewed people in the mob and spent time with people who are in the underworld. They're just terrific guys and lots of fun, but they're violent. It's a business, and I think it was a business for Pete Gusenberg. It's a business to *win* for John

Kreese, but it's also a higher . . . It's about a level of morality and conviction. He doesn't get rich in the dojo. In the end of season two of *Cobra Kai*, he takes over the dojo. It's not about that. He didn't take over the dojo so that he can put more money in his bank. He took over the dojo because Billy Zabka, Johnny Lawrence, violated the concept, the integrity of Cobra Kai and became somewhat soft.

So if you could [we] actually compare [the two], I don't think that Pete Gusenberg or any torpedo who goes *soft* can make a living at all. I don't think John Kreese is a killer, but he could be for survival. Pete Gusenberg or any hitman is a killer by choice.

Good distinction.

What did you learn from working with Roger Corman?

Well, I learned about his economics. I remember going up there and chatting with him about *Firehawk* in 1991, 1992. I was sitting at his desk. He was on the phone when I arrived, and I was listening to the phone call. I could tell from the dialogue that it was about another movie that was going over budget. As soon as he got off the phone, he went and shut off the air conditioner because the movie in that location was over budget.

[laughs] Wow.

~~So he was gonna save money that afternoon with the air conditioner off because that other movie was over budget.~~

I hope the air conditioning isn't still off.

I thought it was classic. I cracked up hysterically, but I didn't tell him why. So many

great people worked for this guy. Jonathan Demme, Francis Coppola. I've got the VHSs [versions] of all these movies. It was really a great playground for the young director. Nowadays, kids make movies with the iPhones and all that. In those days, you had a *crew*. In those days, he [Corman] financed movies that weren't expensive, but I think you got a better education in those days as a would-be director. He would let actors direct. I just thought that for me, as an actor, it was a great training ground. I think that you learn what not to do. You want a better dressing room. You want a few of the things you get later on in your career. You don't even know that the dressing room is second rate because it just *is*.

When you turn on that set and you're doing the action[,] ~~and~~ you're doing the shooting and the falling and all that, as a young actor or a young director, it's heaven. You're getting to create your own destiny and your own art form. A lot of people owe him a great deal of thanks.

When you worked with Stallone again on *Rambo: First Blood Part II*, did the two of you ever talk about those earlier experiences with Corman?

[note: In the final, there is another paragraph that appears before the following paragraph. I reverse the order of the two paragraphs in the final. I mention that because otherwise the next paragraph in this draft seems completely disconnected from the question once I eliminate the "No, but" a few lines down. Even with those two words left intact, the following answer seems more to use the initial question as a jumping off point to talk about something else, which is why I move content around in the final. That way Kove gives a more thorough response to the question and then dives into the Robert Carradine content. Flipping the paragraph order also lends a more structured sense to the answer because Kove will move through his answer chronologically in the final version. Another strategy would have been to create a new question or two.]

~~No, but~~ I talked about the earlier experience when I went to do the new version of *Kung Fu, Kung Fu: The Legend Continues* with Robert Carradine in the early 1990s. I played the Shadow Assassin. I was Carradine's nemesis, and I was stronger than he was. I was in a black duster and would come up only for the premier episodes of the three years **[that the new *Kung Fu* was on]** and create havoc in his life. One day at nine in the morning on the set, which made it six in the morning in L.A., he and I decided to call Roger and tell him that we wanted to do a remake of *Death Race 2000.* We called him up on the phone and he couldn't believe it. Both of us were on the phone. David, bless his soul, has a bottle of Hires root beer, and Hires root beer is brown. He's got this bottle, and it's clear liquid, so he was drinking at nine in the morning, Toronto time. We called Roger. Roger laughed at us and said, "Oh, how are you guys,[?]" blah, blah, blah. "Alright, sure, we'll do it" and he hung up on us. We had such a good time ~~conceiving all the fun we had working with him~~ because he and Stallone had the lead in *Death Race 2000.* Then, David and I became good friends after that. It was fun reminiscing there.

Sly and I didn't reminisce too much about **[the Corman movies]** —. We reminisced about Kuno Sponholtz, and we reminisced about *The Lords of ~~Discipline~~*, [**Flatbush**] a movie he [**Stallone**] did. He tried to get Perry King out and get me in there. He and I spent a lot of time [**together**] ~~…~~ because he and I lived next to each other in 1974 when we both got out there [**to Hollywood**]. We had a lot of good times. I see him every six months. We talk a lot about *The Expendables*. He asked me if I wanted to be in it and I said, "Yeah," and then he didn't write the last one, so we'll see what happens.

When you were making *Death Race 2000*, how did you think it would end up performing in the box office and what did you think people's opinion of it would be?

In those days, I didn't know. I really didn't know because I wasn't repulsed by it.

When I did *The Last House on the Left* a couple of years earlier, I never liked that movie. I never liked it. I thought it was too gruesome. I was asked to play Krug, the lead guy, the chainsaw beast who kills the girls and all this stuff. I bowed out and David Hesse was my good friend at the time. I dressed him up in a sweater and I brought him ~~into that~~ to meet Sean Cunningham and Wes Craven. It was Wes Craven's first movie, and David got the part~~,~~ and ~~he~~ also wrote the music.

But I never got a real negative feeling from *Death Race 2000* until I saw it in its entirety. Then I realized . . . I love babies so much. I have a two-year-old grandson and a four-year-old granddaughter. I could never conceive some of those things ~~of the~~ [**like**] car[**s**] hitting ~~the~~ babies, and ~~there was a bomb in it~~ [**bombs disguised as babies**].

[I'm also thinking about the connection between Nero and Kreese regarding exploding children. Nero is undone by his lack of compassion or empathy when he runs over what he thinks is a baby, and, according to your backstory for Kreese, his soldiers are literally killed by an exploding child and that earlier, more innocent or empathetic version of Kreese is figuratively killed by the kid with the dynamite.]

I'm thinking, too, about how they're both earning or focused on earning points in their movie's respective sports. Nero's method is driving over innocent pedestrians who are mostly unwilling and unarmed. John Kreese's method—at least within the tournaments—involves willing participants who are more or less equally matched and fighting hand-to-hand, not

body-to-car. At the same time, it seems that neither believes in showing mercy.

~~My character~~ **[Nero]** going after a baby carriage . . . Some of that to me was over the top, but it **[*Death Race 2000*]** was far more entertaining as a whole movie. But you look at it as an actor, look at the actions of the individual character, and it's a little over the top.

Now ~~you're~~ **[I'm]** doing other things like ~~I did~~ the Tarantino movie and *Cobra Kai* and it's a whole different world because ~~you're~~ **[I'm]** more seasoned, and yet you've gotta go through the Roger Corman school of learning what's appropriate and what's not as a talent. You make mistakes, you rectify them, and he give you an arena to make the mistakes.

Is it okay if I ask you one more question?

~~Yeah~~ **[Sure]. [note: *Yeah* could sound unenthusiastic. *Sure* conveys the enthusiasm in Kove's voice.]** Go ahead.

~~We talked about how you studied martial arts and~~ **I read that you have a black belt in karate [and continue to train in martial arts]. What lessons or principles can you apply from karate to filmmaking, Corman, acting, and/or Hollywood?**

Discipline.

Sheer discipline. **[note: I gave these three words two paragraphs to try to express the intensity with which Kove said them.]**

Karate is about discipline. Karate is about focus. Karate, according to Mr. Miyagi, was defined as a defensive art. John Kreese defines it as an offensive sport. There are some people that if they win in the tournament, it's enough. John Kreese's concept is it's not about just the tournament; it's about **[making sure]** that your enemy, your opponent doesn't get up because on the street if you let someone get up, you endanger your life. He applies the same thing from the streets to a tournament.

But in either case, acting or directing for Roger Corman or anyone, it's discipline. It's discipline to do your homework. It's discipline to do your backstories. Discipline to really have a couple of alternatives as an actor to play with. If something doesn't work out, you have a plan B, plan C. ~~I think in the arena of making a movie, any movie,~~

[M]~~my~~ son's doing a movie. He's got a great movie coming out called *D-Day*. His name is Jesse Cove, terrific ~~little~~ actor. He and

Weston Cage, Nic's kid, ~~try[?]~~ [are] leads in ~~this movie~~ *D-Day*, ~~which is out September 13 in the theaters~~. It's a great story about two-hundred rangers destroying howitzers that were about to bomb Omaha Beach, about to destroy the ships coming in. He did a great job, and yet he just is off now doing a movie for nothing. I told him, "Jesse, this is the lead. It's a good script. Go do it." He said, "Dad, I don't want to work for nothing." I said, "Go do it. They'll take care of you. I've worked for the producer two other times, ~~once in London as a pilot for a piece.~~" I spoke to ~~him~~ [Jesse] today and he's having a great time. He didn't want to do it—no money.

I think any arena where you like the material, where you like the role [it's worth doing it], whether it's Roger Corman or you're working for John Avildsen or you're working for Michael Bay or Quentin—~~that movie had more trucks on the set than trucks for fruit, trucks for ice cream, trucks for popcorn~~. I didn't get paid much money on that movie, but to work for Quentin, be in a movie with Quentin . . . You learn that early on when you're with Roger. [If] [y] You have the opportunity to exercise your craft, whether you're a director or a prop man or you're an actor starting out, you go for it. That's the discipline we have to use as young actors. I think young actors have to use it, and even I would use it now.

If a project came along that I loved, and I was getting paid nine dollars, [—]like a Western somewhere, [—] I'd go do it because you only can benefit ~~by~~ [from] it, man. You can only benefit ~~by it~~. The through-line of all of this is discipline. When you have the opportunity to exercise your discipline, make it happen.

~~38:51 As bizarre as that movie was [DR 2000], it was so much fun to work for him~~

So I did *Capone*, *Death Race 2000*, *Baby Face Nelson*, and *Firehawk*. Did I do anything in between?

There was also . . .

Oh, yeah. The series! I did the series! That's right. I did . . .

Black Scorpion.

Yeah, what the hell was the character's name?

Firearm.

Firearm. Right! I took my ten-year-old son on the set. He had a ball. I've got so many photographs of that show. The chick was fantastic. She went off, left her career after that. She left to do something with movies with a preacher up in Oregon. But she was great-looking. It was the first series I think ~~he~~ [Corman] did.

We kept going back and shooting more stuff. I had a great time. ~~I really had a good time~~ on that show. So many celebrities came and did pickup shots and we all bumped into each other. Yeah, that was . . . My kids were ten, so that must've been about 2000.

2001.

Yeah. That would have been the last thing I did for him, I think.

Did you ever have the opportunity to work on any of his other projects and you said no, the timing didn't work out, or otherwise declined, or were those the only offers you got from Corman?

[*long pause*] There might have been a couple of others. I can't remember. Those five are the ones I really remember stories from. ~~I don't think so.~~ **[note: I would probably leave this in now].**

I remember the worst refusal I ever ~~did~~ **[made]**, but it wasn't a Roger Corman movie. ~~It was *Tom Horn* and I was going to play . . .~~ **[Y]**~~y~~ou talk about big mistakes. I was offered ~~to play~~ **[the part of]** Gentleman Jim Corbett, a week's work, with Steve McQueen in *Tom Horn*, the last Western he made. He was my idol. I'll never forget it. What a dumb thing. I arrived in New York to see my parents. The phone call came in that *day*. I didn't want to upset my parents and leave the next morning because I had to if I took the part, and I passed on it. Then he passed away about a year later. That was the *worst* decision I ever made in my life. The worst—as far as the career goes.

[note: It was tempting to see if I could take that last sentence as an opening to ask what the worst mistake was that Kove ever made outside of his professional career. However, my felt sense in the moment was that this might have been pushing too far, and I wasn't sure he would be receptive to it. Also, I wanted to talk with him about *The Karate Kid* a little bit more. That subject I knew he would be receptive to because he has been quite open to talking about it and, unprompted, he often brings the movie up during the interview in relation to something else. Also, I didn't get a sense of being pushed for time, but I also knew we were only going to have so long to talk. Did I want to spend that opportunity getting him to dredge up uncomfortable and deeply personal feelings about his life that might cause him to withdraw or did I want to spend the time talking about an experience that he felt good about and a film that I love?]

The only thing I wanted to add is I know the main focus of this is supposed to be Roger Corman and his stuff with New World Pictures, but I really love *The Karate Kid* and your work in it. I saw it when it first came out in the theater when I was a kid. It resonated with me then, and it's stayed with me through my whole adult life. Just to be a fan for a second, I just wanted to tell you that and how much I enjoyed it.

Well, thank you very much. That's very kind of you.

Cobra Kai, of course, picks up with a lot of that story and those characters.

Can we talk a little bit about that and your role?

Absolutely. I enter in episode ten, and I set up season two. It's a great show. It's not white hats and black hats like the movie. My character is written with some vulnerability, lots of versatility. You'll end up binging it. You'll binge five episodes a night. It's thirty minutes long. It's brilliantly written. Ralph Macchio is in it and William Zabka who played Johnny Lawrence. He kind of starred in it. They're the two stars in it. I come in episode ten, season one, and I blow the whole thing wide open. We are the most streamed show on the planet. It doesn't matter what they are; they all come in second. The only show watched more than us was a network show called *Game of Thrones*.

[Wow!] [note: I'm not a big fan of exclamation marks for several reasons. People tend to overuse them. What gets overused gets devalued and loses power and significance (If we held the Olympics every year and there were ten types of medals instead of three, being an Olympic medalist would not be as meaningful). People also rely on the exclamation mark to indicate—rather than show—a sense of excitement, enthusiasm, or importance. Overuse of the exclamation mark is getting so bad that when I have responded to a question and punctuate my response with a period, people often ask me if something is wrong. While I don't think "Yes, there is a meeting on the schedule" requires an exclamation mark, apparently we are all supposed to be super-excited about everything all the time—"I had lunch today! Grass is green! Water is wet!" In this situation, I used the exclamation mark. "Wow" with a period sounds flat and may read sarcastically. Also, as you see, I don't use the exclamation mark much. It's not that I am completely against the exclamation mark; I just think it should be used sparingly, if

at all, and only when the content really calls for and earns it or needs it.]

That's how good this show is. So just get it and watch it. You'll love it. They bring in flashbacks, and these cats are so smart. ~~They~~ **[The three writers]** went to the archives of Columbia **[Pictures]**, ~~the three writers,~~ and they got angles and cuts from scenes that were in the movie but they were different outtakes, so they were different angles. So when you're watching these episodes and you see flashbacks of the movie, it looks like you remember it, but they're different angles.

Oh, that's so cool. [note: At this point, I trust readers to realize the tone I said this in, especially since I ended my last response with an exclamation mark. I could have added a short comment to reinforce or show that tone, but I trust the reader in this case.]

That's the kind of research these guys did. ~~Why wait? Just order it now, and then cancel your subscription.~~ **[note: I thought this sounded a little too much like an advertisement, and it doesn't add anything to the content.]** You can watch twenty episodes of nothing but terrific writing and **[it will bring up]** a lot of great memories for you. It's good stuff. It's *really*, really good.

Okay, my friend, take care of yourself. Call Steve **[Carver]** and tell Steve if you had a good time. He always likes to hear about my activity.

[Alright]. Thank you so much. I'll give you a great report.

*

Final Draft Example: Martin Kove

Next, I'll give the final version that I developed and sent to the general editor.

*

What Roger Corman films were you in?

Don't you know? [laughs]

Well, I *know*, but I just wanted to go ahead and get it in the interview.

I got you.

You were in *Capone* and *Death Race 2000*, correct?

Yeah. My first year in Hollywood I did like three movies and eight TV shows. Two of
the three were Corman's. The first one was *Capone* with Ben Gazzara, Sly Stallone, and Susan Blakely. That was directed by Steve Carver. Then I went off and did *Death Race 2000*.

Those were the two movies for New World Pictures.

Yes. Let me tell you some of these great stories.

Yes, please.

In *Capone*, I was playing this guy, Peter Gusenberg, who died in the St. Valentine's Day Massacre. It was fun playing a real-life guy. I liked doing research and all that for these characters. Pete Gusenberg was in the O'Banion Gang, the North Side Gang, which was a bunch of the Polish and Irishmen fighting against Al Capone.

I wanted to have a really cool gun. There was a scene where I walk up after ten cars have shot the shit out of this café with machine guns trying to kill Frank Nitti and Al Capone, which happened in real life. I stop. I get out of my car. I wanted to have something different. Everybody else was using Thompsons. I went into Stembridge Gun Rentals, and I had the idea of this character always using antique weapons to kill people. He was using things like World War I flare guns. This guy Pete Gusenberg always had weird shit that he wanted to use. He was a torpedo, which is what they called it in those days. It's another word for a hitman. I went in Stembridge, went around with a shopping cart, and I got all these great, great weapons. *Great* weapons.

I wanted to have a .30 caliber machine gun removed from the tripod and draped over my arm. The director went for it. I rented that and all of a sudden Roger comes up and says, "What's this?" And I said, "Well, I wanted to make the guy, you know . . ." Roger says, "Do you know what this will cost?" He says, "You can have *one*. You just have a Thompson machine gun." I said, "Yeah, but everybody else has got a Thompson." Roger says, "No." He calls over the director, and then he leaves me alone with the director. I say, "Steve, look, you gotta at least give me two Thompsons, one on each arm. I shoot the shit. I get out of my car. It's a total definitive scene." Steve said, "I've got two cameras shooting out on the street, two cameras shooting into the café. If one of these guns jams, we're in trouble. If just one jams, and there's no bullets coming out of it, there's a problem. So you can have one Thompson, which is jam-proof, and you hold it steady, and that's how you're gonna get it." Bottom line: It was a great scene, and I only got one Thompson.

That other thing that happened in *Capone* was that the prop guy gave me a double-barrel shotgun, and it's draped over the open window of a car I'm about to use to shoot one of our enemies. I'm in the driver's seat. Steve comes out to talk. The double-barrel shotgun is aimed at his throat, and he's giving me a direction. I don't know what I was thinking. I actually didn't think there were any shells in there. I answer him and finish the direction, put him at ease that I'm gonna do what he told me to do. I drop the shotgun down across my lap. BOOM! BOOM! It blew giant holes the size of basketballs with these blanks. It was pointblank against the inside door of the car. If they had gone off on his throat, he'd be dead. It would have blown half his throat off. It was *unbelievable*. Ever since then I check the guns I use five times.

So that was two stories. The third story I found out years later while doing another movie that pertained to Capone, *Baby Face Nelson*. C. Thomas Howell played Baby Face Nelson and I played John Dillinger. This is 1996; we're jumping ahead chronologically because it's related. There's a scene where we rob a bank in the 1996 version of *Baby Face Nelson*. I'm in an open convertible, and guys from a rival gang are chasing me. I've got a mustache, blue suit, and

I'm standing up and shooting shells out of the back of the convertible with the top down. I never saw who was chasing me.

A year later, *Baby Face Nelson* gets released. I watch the movie and all of a sudden, the guy chasing me appears in a tan suit. I have a picture of me in a tan suit. I recognize the car and the whole deal. I said to myself, "This looks really familiar." I zoom in with my VHS remote, and there it is: Marty Kove chasing Marty Kove. Corman had taken footage from *Capone* where many times I was hanging out of an old Model T shooting at someone. It was me, and only I would know this because I zoomed in with the remote to see myself, Martin Kove, hanging out of that car, shooting at Martin Kove twenty years later playing John Dillinger.

That's great! Classic.

Unbelievable. *Unbelievable.* I have both movies now so I can show it to people. I said to myself, "I wonder if Roger did that to pay homage to me, literally as a joke, as a very inside joke that only I would catch, or did he do it because he had the stock footage and he owned it and he used it . . ."

To save a buck.

Yeah, which, of course, was what he was always doing. It was incredible when I found that out. So that was jumping to 1996.

Now, I'm moving back to *Death Race 2000*, which was February of 1975. That was when Sylvester Stallone and I were friends in New York. We had the same personal manager, an old guy named Kuno Sponholtz. Kuno Sponholtz used to get Sly jobs as an usher in the Baronet in different theaters and get me a job as Santa Claus in department stores, so that's the kind of personal manager he was. We knew each other for years. Stallone and I did these two movies back-to-back, *Capone* and *Death Race 2000*. It was a lot of fun. In February of 1975, he's sitting in the motorhome with this red script, so I say, "Sly, what have you got there?" He says, "Ah, it's just a boxing movie I'm trying to make, man. I'm hitting a lot of dead ends." I said, "Good luck with it." So that was February of 1975. He got the movie made. Needless to say, it was *Rocky*.

In 1976, he called me and I was doing a TV series called *Code R*. I was in my first month shooting, and it was my first series in Hollywood.

You had been on episodes of other shows, but this was the first one where you played a character that appeared in multiple episodes.

Right.

I couldn't go to the screening of *Rocky*, and he was pissed off because I was a good friend, and I couldn't go to see his premiere. The bottom line is he doesn't talk to me for *years*. I didn't do anything for Roger in between. It comes *Rambo* time and Stallone puts me in *Rambo: First Blood Part II.*

When you worked with Stallone again on *Rambo: First Blood Part II*, did the two of you ever talk about those earlier experiences with Corman?

Sly and I didn't reminisce too much about the Corman movies. We reminisced about Kuno Sponholtz, and we reminisced about *The Lords of Flatbush*, a movie Stallone did. He tried to get Perry King out and get me in there. He and I spent a lot of time together because he and I lived next to each other in 1974 when we both got out to Hollywood. We had a lot of good times. I see him every six months. We talk a lot about *The Expendables*. He asked me if I wanted to be in it and I said, "Yeah," and then Sly didn't write the last one, so we'll see what happens.

I talked about the earlier experiences with Roger when I went to do the new version of *Kung Fu, Kung Fu: The Legend Continues* with Robert Carradine in the early 1990s. I played the Shadow Assassin. I was Carradine's nemesis, and I was stronger than he was. I was in a black duster and would come up only for the premier episodes of the three years that the new *Kung Fu* was on and create havoc in his life.

One day at nine in the morning on the set, which made it six in the morning in L.A., he and I decided to call Roger and tell him that we wanted to do a remake of *Death Race 2000.* We called him up on the phone, and he couldn't believe it. Both of us were on the phone. David, bless his soul, has a bottle of Hires root beer, and Hires root beer is brown. He's got this bottle, and it's clear liquid, so he was drinking at nine in the morning, Toronto time. We called Roger. Roger laughed at us and said, "Oh, how are you guys?" blah, blah, blah. "Alright, sure, we'll do it" and he hung up on us. We had such a good time because he and Stallone had the lead in *Death Race 2000.* Then, David and I became good friends after that. It was fun reminiscing there.

After *Capone* and *Death Race 2000*, I don't think I did anything for Roger again until 1992. In 1992, I finished *Cagney & Lacey*. I finished all the *Karate Kid* movies. There's a movie called *Firehawk* shooting in the Philippines and Roger's old friend, Cirio Santiago, is directing it. Now, Cirio Santiago has got racehorses. Cirio Santiago couldn't care less about *Firehawk*, but it was a good script and I loved the character. The writer and I used to have to fight Cirio Santiago to do coverage because he would shoot masters all the time just so that he could get out of the set and get back to Manila where his horses were running. It was a long, long journey. I finished the movie. Good cast. I loved it.

I see Roger in Beverly Hills every once in a while. I'll say, "How you doing?" and all that. I never did another movie for him after *Baby Face Nelson*.

That's the history of Roger, and I really had such a good time working with his movies.

How was the pay?

Never made a nickel. I made decent money on *Firehawk*. In those days, I would do movies where I fell in love with the role. If a script was fair, I was arrogant enough to say, "Hey, my performance will make this script better," which of course it never did. Each one of those epics I enjoyed so much for whatever reason.

Please talk about Pete Gusenberg's death in *Capone*.

When I died in the St. Valentine's Day Massacre, all the stunt guys just went down like dominoes in that scene. I spun around, flipped over the chair. I did everything I could to make it a Hamlet death because I did not want to just fall down like all the stunt guys did. I think that's why my knees hurt, my shoulders hurt. Everything on my body is bad because back in those days you didn't have a lot of lines, so you'd try to do great action sequences.

In the extras for *Death Race 2000*, Corman says that "The audition with Martin Kove really was wild." What can you tell us about the audition for *Death Race*?

I'm amazed that he remembers that audition. Did he really say that?

He did. I've got it in quotes because I reviewed the extras last week. So I'm curious what you remember.

I remember that audition very clearly. I went in there after reading the script. Remember, he's Nero the Hero, so I went in there with a character really in that Roman mold. I played it all—walk, gestures, voice. I just thought that was the essence of the character. I felt this Nero the Hero was so over the top. He was so full of himself. It was only a month after, two months after I did *Capone* for Corman, and I was really feeling good as an actor. When you feel good, you take a lot of chances. I thought about Laurence Olivier with Tony Curtis in *Spartacus*. Corman said, "Just take it down a little bit." So I took the vocal pitch down so that the voice wasn't so high. He loved it. He gave me the part. It was great. [*laughs*]

What do you think is the theme or message of *Death Race 2000*?

That's an interesting question. [*pauses*] Such a violent movie. I think the message could

be that if we don't lasso our own humanity now, that ultimately things like *Rollerball* with Jimmy Caan and *Death Race 2000* could actually happen. It's like the rise and fall of the Roman Empire. If you don't arrest some of the lack of humanity, you'll end up with cars hitting babies and people getting points for doing it. It's just the way it is. I think *Death Race 2000* is very pertinent to *now*.

My character John Kreese in *The Karate Kid* feels that kids are babied nowadays. They're *soft*. They get trophies for just participating, and I have a scene like that in season two of *Cobra Kai*. Marty Kove feels that kids who aren't the A players deserve acknowledgement. I'm not sure they deserve the same trophies, participation trophies, as the kid who scored all the goals in soccer. I'm not sure about that, but as far as Nero the Hero goes and a lot of people out there, they think everybody should get a trophy for participating in *life*. I don't think so. You've gotta have a high level of integrity and honesty to get a trophy in life, I think, along with whatever your prowess is.

So you are saying that Nero the Hero and John Kreese are dissimilar in that respect, right?

Yes. They're dissimilar because Nero didn't do anything.

The title of "Hero" for Nero is kind of ironic, then, and unearned in your estimation.

What did Nero do? He drove a car and he hit people. He had no real expertise.

I'm thinking, too, about how they're both earning or focused on earning points in their movie's respective sports. Nero's method is driving over innocent pedestrians who are mostly unwilling and unarmed. John Kreese's method—at least within the tournaments—involves willing participants who are more or less equally matched and fighting hand-to-hand, not

body-to-car. At the same time, it seems that neither believes in showing mercy.

The no-mercy concept for John Kreese is based on his experience in Vietnam. He would go up to a Vietcong boy with his platoon to give the boy chocolate and the kid was laced with dynamite and BOOM. That proved that mercy is for the weak because by showing mercy so many of his good friends died. So he came back, created Cobra Kai and the concept of no mercy, to win—not to lose. Because when he was in Vietnam he was never allowed to win, like so many of our soldiers were not allowed to win. John Kreese was allowed to win in high school and college. He was allowed to win in tournaments, but he wasn't allowed to win as a soldier, which he vowed would never happen again, and certainly not in his dojo.

Do you see any connections between Kreese and Pete Gusenberg from *Capone*?

I don't think John Kreese likes to kill people. I think he would only kill people in Vietnam when it was necessary and they proved dangerous. I think Pete Gusenberg was just a paid gun. It's a business. As actors, we've all interviewed people in the mob and spent time with people who are in the underworld. They're just terrific guys and lots of fun, but they're violent. It's a business, and I think it was a business for Pete Gusenberg. It's a business to *win* for John Kreese, but it's also a higher . . . It's about a level of morality and conviction. He doesn't get rich in the dojo. In the end of season two of *Cobra Kai*, he takes over the dojo. It's not about that. He didn't take over the dojo so that he can put more money in his bank. He took over the dojo because Billy Zabka, Johnny Lawrence, violated the concept, the integrity of Cobra Kai and became somewhat soft.

So if we actually compare the two, I don't think that Pete Gusenberg or any torpedo who goes *soft* can make a living at all. I don't think John Kreese is a killer, but he could be for survival. Pete Gusenberg or any hitman is a killer by choice.

Good distinction.

What did you learn from working with Roger Corman?

Well, I learned about his economics. I remember going up there and chatting with him about *Firehawk* in 1991, 1992. I was sitting at his desk. He was on the phone when I arrived, and I was listening to the phone call. I could tell from the dialogue that it was about another movie that was going over budget. As soon as he got off the phone, he went and shut off the air conditioner to save money because the movie in that location was over budget.

[laughs] Wow. I hope the air conditioning isn't still off.

I thought it was classic. I cracked up hysterically, but I didn't tell him why.

So many great people worked for this guy. Jonathan Demme, Francis Coppola. I've got

the VHS versions of all these movies. It was really a great playground for the young director. Nowadays, kids make movies with the iPhone and all that. In those days, you had a *crew*. In those days, Corman financed movies that weren't expensive, but I think you got a better education in those days as a would-be director. He would let actors direct. I just thought that for me, as an actor, it was a great training ground. I think that you learn what not to do. You want a better dressing room. You want a few of the things you get later on in your career. You don't even know that the dressing room is second rate because it just *is*.

When you turn on that set and you're doing the action, you're doing the shooting, and the falling, and all that, as a young actor or a young director, it's heaven. You're getting to create your own destiny and your own art form. A lot of people owe him a great deal of thanks.

When you were making *Death Race 2000*, how did you think it would perform in the box office, and what did you think people's opinion of it would be?

In those days, I didn't know. I really didn't know. I wasn't repulsed by it.

When I did *The Last House on the Left* a couple of years earlier, I never liked that movie. I never liked it. I thought it was too gruesome. I was asked to play Krug, the lead guy, the chainsaw beast who kills the girls and all this stuff. I bowed out and David Hesse was my good friend at the time. I dressed him up in a sweater and I brought him to meet Sean Cunningham and Wes Craven. It was Wes Craven's first movie, and David got the part and also wrote the music.

But I never got a real negative feeling from *Death Race 2000* until I saw it in its entirety. Then I realized . . . I love babies so much. I have a two-year-old grandson and a four-year-old granddaughter. I could never conceive some of those things like cars hitting babies, and bombs disguised as babies.

I'm also thinking about the connection between Nero and Kreese regarding exploding children. Nero is undone by his lack of compassion or empathy when he runs over what he thinks is a baby, and, according to your backstory for Kreese, his soldiers are literally killed by an exploding child and that earlier, more innocent or empathetic version of Kreese is figuratively killed by the kid with the dynamite.

Nero going after a baby . . . Some of that to me was over the top, but *Death Race 2000* was far more entertaining as a whole movie. But you look at it as an actor, look at the actions of the individual character, and it's a little over the top.

Now I'm doing other things like the Tarantino movie and *Cobra Kai* and it's a whole different world because I'm more seasoned, and yet you've gotta go through the Roger Corman school of learning what's appropriate and what's not as a talent. You make mistakes, you rectify them, and he gives you an arena to make the mistakes.

How did you come to *Once Upon a Time. . . in Hollywood*?

Five years ago, I'm sitting in the Directors Guild and they're having a screening of *Inglourious Basterds*. I wanted to be in *Django Unchained* because I want to work with Tarantino, but I want to do a Western with him. I go to the screening. Five-hundred of my peers are at the Directors Guild. I go there with my girlfriend and there on the day is Brad Pitt, Michael Fassbender, Diane Kruger, and Quentin. I raised my hand to ask a question and Tarantino goes, "Marty Kove! Marty Kove, you're one of my favorite actors. I love you. You starred in this movie, *Firehawk*. It's one of my favorite pictures." Well, *Firehawk* was ultimately a piece of *shit*. The movie didn't get the legs it should have gotten, but the character was great. A moment later, Brad Pitt grabs the mic and says, "And we just watched *The Karate Kid* with my six-year-old daughter, and you've still got it Mr. Kove. You were great. You're a legend in our house." So I feel like a million bucks. I go back into the backroom. My girlfriend is taking pictures with Brad Pitt. Michael Fassbender comes up to me and says, "I love you, man. I've been following your career forever." I said, "Oh, really? Great." This is before Michael Fassbender hits.

I exchange numbers with Tarantino. My night is complete. I'm feeling great, put the top down on my Porsche, lit a cigar, threw a scarf on and a cap. It was freezing that night, but I didn't even feel it because I had Quentin's number. I was gonna call him the next day and say, "Let's have a cigar and talk about doing a Western." Well, I get home and I can't read his handwriting.

Ohhhhhh. What a tough break.

For six months I did everything any actor could do to find this guy's phone number, couldn't get the phone number, and then ultimately he made good on his promise three years later by inviting me to come play in *Once Upon a Time. . . in Hollywood.* I'm in the opening scene. And it's a Western.

Is it okay if I ask you one more question?

Sure. Go ahead.

I read that you have a black belt in karate and continue to train in martial arts.

What lessons or principles can you apply from karate to filmmaking, Corman, acting, and/or Hollywood?

Discipline.

Sheer discipline.

Karate is about discipline. Karate is about focus. Karate, according to Mr. Miyagi, was defined as a defensive art. John Kreese defines it as an offensive sport. There are some people that if they win in the tournament, it's enough. John Kreese's concept is it's not about just the tournament; it's about making sure that your enemy, your opponent, doesn't get up because on the street if you let someone get up, you endanger your life. He applies the same thing from the streets to a tournament.

But in either case, acting or directing for Roger Corman or anyone, it's discipline. It's discipline to do your homework. It's discipline to do your backstories. Discipline to really have a couple of alternatives as an actor to play with. If something doesn't work out, you have a plan B, plan C.

My son's doing a movie. He's got a great movie coming out called *D-Day.* His name is Jesse Cove, terrific actor. He and Weston Cage, Nic's kid, are leads in *D-Day.* It's a great story about two-hundred rangers destroying howitzers that were about to bomb Omaha Beach, about to destroy the ships coming in. He did a great job, and yet he is off now doing a movie for nothing. I told him, "Jesse, this is the lead. It's a good script. Go do it." He said, "Dad, I don't want to work for nothing." I said, "Go do it. They'll take care of you. I've worked for the producer two other times." I spoke to Jesse today and he's having a great time. He didn't want to do it—no money.

I think any arena where you like the material, where you like the role, it's worth doing it, whether it's Roger Corman or you're working for John Avildsen or you're working for Michael Bay or Quentin. I didn't get paid much money on that movie for Quentin, but to work for Quentin, be in a movie with Quentin . . . You learn that early on when you're with Roger. If you have the opportunity to exercise your craft, whether you're a director or a prop man or you're an actor starting out, you go for it. That's the discipline we have to use as young actors. I think young actors have to use it, and even I would use it now.

If a project came along that I loved, and I was getting paid nine dollars—like a Western somewhere—I'd go do it because you only can benefit from it, man. You can only benefit. The through-line of all of this is discipline. When you have the opportunity to exercise your discipline, make it happen.

So I did *Capone, Death Race 2000, Firehawk,* and *Baby Face Nelson.* Did I do anything in between?

There was also . . .

Oh, yeah. The series! I did the series! That's right. I did . . .

Black Scorpion.

Yeah, what the hell was the character's name?

Firearm.

Firearm. Right! I took my ten-year-old son on the set. He had a ball. I've got so many photographs of that show. The chick was fantastic. She went off, left her career after that. She left to do something with movies with a preacher up in Oregon. But she was great-looking. It was the first series I think Corman did.

We kept going back and shooting more stuff. I had a great time on that show. So many celebrities came and did pickup shots and we all bumped into each other. Yeah, that was . . . My kids were ten, so that must've been about 2000.

2001.

Yeah. That would have been the last thing I did for him, I think.

Did you ever have the opportunity to work on any of his other projects and you said no, the timing didn't work out, or you otherwise declined, or were those the only offers you got from Corman?

[*long pause*] There might have been a couple of others. I can't remember. Those five are the ones I really remember stories from.

I remember the worst refusal I ever made, but it wasn't a Roger Corman movie. You talk about big mistakes. I was offered the part of Gentleman Jim Corbett, a week's work, with Steve McQueen in *Tom Horn*, the last Western he made. He was my idol. I'll never forget it. What a dumb thing. I arrived in New York to see my parents. The phone call came in that *day*. I didn't want to upset my parents and leave the next morning because I had to if I took the part, and I passed on it. Then he passed away about a year later. That was the *worst* decision I ever made in my life. The worst—as far as the career goes.

The only thing I wanted to add is I know the main focus of this is supposed to be Roger Corman and his stuff with New World Pictures, but I really love *The Karate Kid* and your work in it. I saw it when it first came out in the theater when I was a kid. It resonated with me then, and it's stayed with me through my whole adult life. Just to be a fan for a second, I just wanted to tell you that and how much I enjoyed it.

Well, thank you very much. That's very kind of you.

Cobra Kai, of course, picks up with a lot of that story and those characters.

Can we talk a little bit about that and your role?

Absolutely. I enter in episode ten, and I set up season two. It's a great show. It's not white hats and black hats like the movie. My character is written with some vulnerability, lots of versatility. You'll end up binging it. You'll binge five episodes a night. Each episode is thirty minutes long. It's brilliantly written. Ralph Macchio is in it and William Zabka who played Johnny Lawrence is, too. They're the two stars in it. I come in episode ten, season one, and I blow the whole thing wide open. We are the most streamed show on the planet. It doesn't matter what they are they all come in second. The only show watched more than us was a network show called *Game of Thrones*.

Wow!

That's how good this show is. So just get it and watch it. You'll love it. They bring in flashbacks, and these cats are so smart. The three writers went to the archives of Columbia Pictures, and they got angles and cuts from scenes that were in the movie but they were different outtakes, so they were different angles. So when you're watching these episodes and you see flashbacks of the movie, it looks like you remember it, but they're different angles.

Oh, that's so cool.

That's the kind of research these guys did.

You can watch twenty episodes of nothing but terrific writing and it will bring up a lot of great memories for you. It's good stuff. It's *really*, really good.

Okay, my friend, take care of yourself. Call Steve Carver and tell Steve if you had a good time. He always likes to hear about my activity.

Alright. Thanks so much. I'll give you a great report.

*

That's the version I submitted. The printed version has some differences someone made after I turned it in. Some of the paragraphs have been moved around. A few comments I put in to help break up long stretches of material were removed. My spacing of paragraphs was altered. The printed interview ends with the paragraph beginning "If a project came along that I loved . . ." Everything after that is cut. I can live with it. I certainly recognized that cutting some of the material was a possibility, and I can't say that the changes are indisputably wrong, but I also can't say looking at them that I think they improve the interview or had to be made; the changes just make the interview different.

In terms of the excised material, I can see it both ways. Much of the non-New World Pictures content was cut from an interview that is supposed to focus on New World Pictures. That makes sense. But then I'm not sure why the information about Kove's son was left in as his son's non-New World Pictures movie strikes me as even less relevant than Kove's non-New World Pictures projects or why the elder Kove's role in *Inglourious Basterds* is more relevant/important than his role in *Cobra Kai*. Maybe the criterion wasn't relevancy but something else, like which stories seemed most interesting. On the other hand, if we examine other removed content, *Black Scorpion* was a Corman project, regrets are interesting, and Kove will always be known primarily for the *Karate Kid* franchise. Perhaps someone just decided they wanted that interview to be shorter for some reason (the collection ended up being 162 pages total, including material such as contributor bios and index, so cutting material to make sure everything could fit in doesn't seem to have been the concern). Maybe the cut was arbitrary. You can read more about this in the "Working with Editors" section, but editors may or may not review, discuss, and/or seek your agreement with changes they want to make. Sometimes editors communicate and work with you to develop the final piece and sometimes you turn in the interview and the next time you see it again is in its final, published form. In this case, it was the latter. I'm not sure what the editorial method or thought process was beyond my own in this case, but the Martin Kove interview is published now. In either version, it's a good interview and I'm glad I did it.

If you happen to have or pick up that volume of interviews, you can compare the final version in this book to the final version in that collection and form your own opinions. As for me, on to the next project . . .

Working from Video

Although I have never conducted an interview via video, I have transcribed from video. The situation was that Mark Sikes and Marty Langford interviewed John Vulich for their *Doomed!* documentary about Robert Corman's unreleased *The Fantastic Four*. The interview is about thirty-three minutes long, so obviously most of that didn't make it into the documentary due to time constraints. Sikes and Langford generously offered to let me use the video footage for my own book about that Fantastic Four film. They sent me a passworded link to the video. I consider myself a fast typist and while I know a few people who can accurately type someone's words out as quickly as they are speaking them, I am not one of those people. I have to stop and start a good bit. The problem with transcribing from video is that, unlike stopping mid-recording with a voice recorder, it's very tough to pick back up exactly where you left off on services such as Vimeo and YouTube. As usual, I stopped frequently, and I expended unnecessary time and effort trying to get back to the exact point I left off at.

I'm sure there are other solutions, but I decided to let the video play on my iPad while I set up each of my recorders about a foot away on either side of the iPad. I set everything up in a spare room, closed the door, and tried to avoid making any loud noises that might be picked up and obscure or drown out any of Vulich's interview. I pressed play and came back about around thirty-three minutes later. I checked the start of the interview and fast-forwarded to random parts, including the final minute, just to be sure the recorders copied everything. It all worked just fine. One other advantage to copying everything over to my own equipment was that I didn't have to worry about the password expiring, the video disappearing, or anything else that I would have needed to bother Sikes and Langford over.

While I am sure they would have helped, I try not to ask people to do the exact same thing that they have already done for me. For example, waiting too long and letting a password or link expire, losing emails, not reading emails, not responding to emails asking basic and necessary questions that could be easily and quickly answered, or misplacing files because of lack of organization wastes everyone's time and energy. Again, I see that as part of being professional. Although we all make mistakes and forget things on occasion, if it's a habit, we start to appear incompetent, inattentive, unappreciative, scattered, negligent, and other such descriptors that do not encourage people to work on our behalf and give us assistance.

If Someone Offers You Material, Know Its Source

I had an unusual situation in which the interviewee sent me a typed interview and told me that I could use whatever I wanted to use from it. This was after we finished our own interview. Having a complete unpublished interview sitting around struck me as a little strange but I didn't think all that much of it at the time. I performed a quick check on Google, didn't find anything, and decided it was "clean," as in unpublished but usable. I found 396 words of content I wanted to use from it, so I added those in. Later, I ordered a recent collection of interviews dealing with a similar genre because I wanted to see what I could reverse engineer and learn from that collection for my Fantastic Four collection. I picked a book published with BearManor Media—the same publisher for *Forsaken*—so that I could have a concrete example for how to format the book as a whole. Much to my surprise, I found that same interview word-for-word. If I hadn't caught that, I don't know that much harm would have been done but that is mainly because I picked a book from the same publisher. I hope I could have explained it was an ignorant but honest mistake and that I used relatively little from that interview in my interview (under 8%, but still significant).

I learned a few important lessons from that near-collision. While the interviewee never said it was unpublished or told me that it was published, they probably should have mentioned that it was published, and I definitely should have asked if any of it had been used anywhere else. Be sure of the source of anything anyone offers you and don't assume, as I did, that just because you can't find it or some mention of it on the internet that it hasn't been published somewhere. I did have enough sense to keep the two interviews—the one I conducted and the one I was sent—separate. I made a separate file for the one I was sent and I made a duplicate of it with the parts I planned to use bolded. When I realized that interview was not unpublished, going back to that file with the bolded pieces made it very easy to go back into my interview, locate the parts I had added in from the other interview, and remove them. After I removed those words, I still had over 5,200 words. If I had been struggling to generate content, those 396 words would have meant a lot more. There was one small piece of information I did want to include, so I referenced it with a paraphrase in a later interview with someone else. I said something like, "I read somewhere that . . ." and, of course, that was true. And to answer the final question you might be wondering, no, I didn't tell the interviewee about it. In fact, this is the first time I've ever said anything about it publicly. I believe they were only trying to help me, and, again, it was my responsibility to ask about the interview's origin, use, and destination. I learned a good lesson and although I didn't reprint parts of the interview, I still learned some valuable pieces of information that served me well in other, intangible ways.

Don't look a gift house in the mouth, but know what stable it comes from and learn its lineage.

How to Structure a Collection of Interviews

Every collection of interviews has a theme or some sort of organizing principle. It might be a subject such as a person, a company, a genre, a medium, an era, or a critical theory. However, we still need to structure or sequence those interviews. The order in which you complete the interviews is not necessarily the order in which you will present the interviews. There are a few orders that we can immediately consider. A narrative method of organization is one possibility. There may be an overall story you are trying to tell or that the finished collection suggests. Think beginning, middle, end, climax, plot, conflict, and characters. You can also use a chronological structure. Again, this may not coincide with the order in which you conducted the interviews. Take a film company, for example. A chronological order might the follow the order in which the company made their movies or it might follow the order in which the people who made the movies joined the company. One more idea is to try to tell the story of the company from start to finish and order interviews accordingly.

I would not advise ranking the interviews from worst to best and placing them in the collection according to that order. *Worst* and *best* are terms like *quality, excellence,* or *improvement* that can be hard to define, can be context-dependent, and vary wildly from person to person. What's best or worst to you might or might not seem best or worst to your readership; your sense of best and worst could even be the opposite of everyone else's. Even if your sense of best parallels that of your readers, beginning with what you deem to be the weakest or least-strong material gets the book off to a weak start. If folks are holding a physical copy, they may flip around, start at the beginning, or jump to names that catch their attention. However, more and more people's first contact with a book is on Amazon. The "look inside" or browse feature generally lets people see some of the beginning of the book and maybe some of the end (in books with an index, the index may occupy some of that end preview). Since the middle content is scooped out, that can be the spot to place less essential or weaker interviews. If you are going to arrange interviews according to which ones you think are "best," I would suggest thinking of a V pattern. Start with the strongest ones, put the not-as-strong ones in the middle, and then work back up. You may not strictly rank them as one, two, three, and so on but you might divide them into three roughly equal groups: best (gold), okay (bronze), and good (silver). Notice in that ranking, the strongest material appears first and the lowest-ranked material appears in the middle. I'd place the strongest two interviews first. This was my advice before Amazon became ubiquitous, but Amazon's place in the market only solidifies my opinion.

No matter what method you use, I advise creating a strong start. Even in an era where listeners tend more to listen to songs instead of albums, artists still frontload their albums with their strongest or some of their strongest material. Placing all of the weaker material at the end can create a sense of the collection gradually losing power, like a top or spinning coin wobbling more and more until it topples over, which is why I also reject the order of ordering material from strongest to weakest. We don't want the collection to seem like a gradually deflating balloon that's lost all of its air and lift by the end.

Now, I'll take you through my process for organizing *Forsaken*. I didn't really worry about the order until I had all of the interviews finished. When I started, I did not know all of the interviews I would end up with, new interviewees popped up, and at a certain point I gave up on certain people that either I didn't know how to contact or who never responded. Furthermore, I did not know beforehand how good—as abstract a term as *good* can be—a particular interview would turn out to be. What I decided to do is try to stack the interviews in such a way as to tell the overall story of *The Fantastic Four* through the words of those I interviewed. To do that, arranging the interviews chronologically made the most sense. Basically, I would try to tell the story of the film's origins, its making, and what happened with it afterwards. Narrative and chronological are not the same thing, but they are closely related. If you present something through a series of steps in order of when they occurred, you often end up with a story. If you tell a story, the story will consist of a sequence of events ordered by their occurrence in time. However, for *Forsaken*, using a chronological arrangement would not reflect the order in which I conducted the interviews.

First, I'll list the interviews in the order that I conducted them:

Oley Sassone (director)
Jay Underwood (actor)
Carl Ciarfalio (actor)
Joseph Culp (actor)
Mark Sikes (casting assistant and producer of *Doomed*)
Rebecca Staab (actor)
Michael Bailey Smith (actor)
Roger Corman (co-executive producer)
Ivan Kander (Lucky 9 Studios)
Craig Nevius (screenplay)
Alex Hyde-White (actor)
Kat Green (actor)
Mick Strawn (production design)
Pete Von Sholly (storyboards)
Wurst brothers (music)
Everett Burrell (costumes)
David Keith Miller (actor)
Glenn Garland (film editing)
John Vulich (costumes)
Lloyd Kaufman (Troma Entertainment)
Mark Parry (director of photography)
Robert Alan Beuth (actor)
Chris Gore (on-set journalist)
Chris Walker III (*Fantastic Four*)
Chris Walker (director of animation)

Robert Ito (journalist). Ito generously gave me full and unpublished interviews he conducted with Bernd Eichinger (co-executive producer) and Stan Lee (co-creator of the Fantastic Four).

Next, I'll list the interviews in the order in which they appear in *Forsaken*. I also add a number beside each one that shows its place according to the order in which I originally conducted each interview:

Lloyd Kaufman (Troma Entertainment) (20)
Craig Nevius Part I (screenplay) (10)
Chris Gore (on-set journalist) (23)
Mick Strawn (production design) (13)
Pete Von Sholly (storyboards) (14)
Chris Walker III (*Fantastic Four*) (24)
Chris Walker (director of animation) (25)

Everett Burrell (costumes) (16)
John Vulich (costumes) (19)
Mark Parry (director of photography) (21)
Wurst brothers (music) (15)
Oley Sassone (director) (1)
Carl Ciarfalio (actor) (3)
Jay Underwood (actor) (2)
Rebecca Staab (actor) (6)
Michael Bailey Smith (actor) (7)
Kat Green (actor) (12)
Alex Hyde-White (actor) (11)
Joseph Culp (actor) (4)
David Keith Miller (actor) (17)
Robert Alan Beuth (actor) (22)
Glenn Garland (film editing) (18)
Craig Nevius Part II (screenplay) (10)
Mark Sikes (casting assistant and producer of *Doomed*) (5)
Roger Corman (co-executive producer) (8)
Bernd Eichinger (co-executive producer) via Robert Ito (26)
Ivan Kander (Lucky 9 Studios) (9)
Stan Lee (co-creator of the Fantastic Four) via Robert Ito
   (26)

As you can see from both lists, the order in which I conducted the interviews and the order in which they appear in *Forsaken* vary greatly.

Now, I'll go through each person's name as they appear in *Forsaken* and explain their placement. **Lloyd Kaufman** (Troma Entertainment) appeared in the *Doomed* documentary and recounted Eichinger, who had the film rights to the Fantastic Four, contacting him about making *The Fantastic Four*. He's a cool and interesting character. I thought his interview stood out and makes for a good opening interview. Also, we talked at the end of his interview about my thinking behind how I structured *Forsaken,* so that was another good reason to put his interview first. **Craig Nevius** (screenplay) and I talked for several hours. He was there almost from the beginning and had some interesting post-*The Fantastic Four* related history to talk about. I divided his lengthy interview into two sections: before and after *The Fantastic Four.* **Chris Gore** (on-set journalist) was present during filming and then went his own way. I knew he needed to appear early on. Also, of these first three interviews, I thought the interviews with Kaufman and Nevius were strongest.

At this point, having covered the early and pre-history of *The Fantastic Four*, I start moving through interviews with people who worked on the film but were not in the film. **Mick Strawn** (production design) provided a very thorough and funny interview. A veteran in the industry, he also had some interesting thoughts about and experiences with filmmaking. He gave a frank and unfiltered appraisal of *The Fantastic Four*. He put me in touch with **Pete Von Sholly** (storyboards) at the end of our interview, so Strawn naturally transitions to Sholly.

As I discussed earlier, I compared the credits list of *The Fantastic Four* with *Fantastic Four* to see if anybody had worked on both films. I found one person—Chris Walker. However, after I contacted him, I also discovered that there are two Chris Walkers who had worked separately on each film but just happened to have the same name. Neither knew about the other. I still included an interview built from my correspondence with **Chris Walker III** (*Fantastic Four*). I thought this set up the interview with the **Chris Walker** (director of animation) who had worked on *The Fantastic Four*. The first Chris Walker had some good thoughts on the Fantastic Four franchise as a whole, and I thought including a related interview with the "wrong" Chris Walker would create anticipation for the following interview with the "right" Chris Walker. Next up is **Everett Burrell** (costumes). He and **John Vulich** (costumes) worked together and I know there was some sort of falling out because Burrell told me ahead of the interview that was one of the things he wanted to talk about. Vulich had passed, but Mark Sikes who made the *Doomed* documentary about *The Fantastic Four* had interviewed Vulich. For time reasons, most of that interview was not included in the documentary, but Sikes generously allowed me to use it for my project. After this, I finished with **Mark Parry** (director of photography), the **Wurst brothers** (music), and capped this first third of interviews with **Oley Sassone** (director). I thought Sassone would be a good transition from people who worked on—but were not in—the film to the actual actors. I also put him last in the first-third of the interviews because I was working up to him.

The middle-third of the collection features interviews with the actors. My basic thinking was to build up to the leader of the "good side" and the chief villain—Mister Fantastic and Doctor Doom. I began with **Carl Ciarfalio** (The Thing). He gave a solid, very "keep-it-real" interview and since he expressed a sense of being a bit over-looked or neglected, I decided to place him first. **Jay Underwood** (Johnny Storm / The Human Torch) was next. Then, we have **Rebecca Staab** (Susan Storm / The Invisible Girl). Her interview is very positive and upbeat. **Michael Bailey Smith** (Ben Grimm) really opened up and let himself be vulnerable during our interview. **Kat Green** (Alicia Masters) appears next. I didn't want to begin with her but I wanted to include her in the procession of characters on the "good side," so I went ahead and placed her interview before the one with **Alex Hyde-White** (Reed Richards / Mister Fantastic) who is the team leader. Green asks about making an audiobook from *Forsaken* with Hyde-White's audio company, Punch Audio, so that made a good segue into his interview (it's another story, but indeed Punch Audio eventually produced and released that audiobook). **Joseph Culp** (Victor Von Doom / Doctor Doom) appears next and then we move to one of Doom's underlings, **David Keith Miller** (Trigorin), and finish with **Robert Alan Beuth** (Dr. Hauptman). Even though he played a villain, Beuth exuded optimism and positivity. I liked ending this section of interviews on that upbeat note.

Another order I thought about included placing Ciarfalio directly before Staab because he probably had one of the starkest takes on the whole experience and Staab had the most positive take. Placing them together would have brought out that contrast even more. Her interview had to be after his, however, because I brought up some specific points to her that Ciarfalio and I had talked about. Ultimately, while Underwood gave a great interview, I thought Ciarfalio's was stronger and should be first. Another idea I considered was placing Bailey's and Ciarfalio's interviews back-to-back. The thing—no pun intended—I like about that order is that they essentially split a role. Bailey gave a very, very strong interview so placing him first in the sequence of actors would have worked. I considered closing with Miller instead of Beuth, but I liked the contrast of having one of Doctor Doom's henchmen following directly after Doctor Doom. I thought about putting Miller before Culp, so that the henchman opens for the leader, or using the order of Beuth, Miller, and Culp to build up to the leader, but I still like the idea of having the heroic mastermind and the villainous mastermind back-to-back. Even though I decided not to use it, the following order is probably my second choice:

Carl Ciarfalio (The Thing)
Michael Bailey Smith (Ben Grimm)
Rebecca Staab (Susan Storm / The Invisible Girl)
Jay Underwood (Johnny Storm / The Human Torch)
Kat Green (Alicia Masters)
Alex Hyde-White (Reed Richards / Mister Fantastic)
Robert Alan Beuth (Dr. Hauptman)
David Keith Miller (Trigorin)
Joseph Culp (Victor Von Doom / Doctor Doom)

From here, we move to the final-third of the collection focusing on folks who were involved in finishing the film and its life after production ended. I began with **Glenn Garland** (film editing) and moved to **Craig Nevius** Part II (screenplay). Part II focuses on matters after *The Fantastic Four*. **Mark Sikes** (casting assistant for *The Fantastic Four* and producer of *Doomed*) was one of the first people I talked to. Placing him toward the end makes sense since he has a wide view of the timeline and events and made the documentary about the film. From an outside perspective, the crown jewel of the collection might be **Roger Corman** (co-executive producer). After all, he is the one who made the deal with Bernd Eichinger to make the film and has gotten much of the blame for the film's shelving. If there is anyone who knows the truth of what happened, we would assume Corman is the keeper of the secret. His interview is, in a sense, the climax, so I wanted that to come late in the collection.

Corman would have been an appropriate and logical person to finish the collection. However, I made a different decision. Robert Ito interviewed **Bernd Eichinger** (co-executive producer) and Stan Lee years earlier for a piece on *The Fantastic Four*. A few quotes from those interviews appear in the article, but the majority of both interviews remained unpublished until *Forsaken*. The transcriptions are pretty rough because Ito was just trying to get quotes for his article and didn't intend to create a full and finished interview. I was hesitant to change very much because obviously I couldn't get input from Eichinger and Stan Lee who have passed on. I placed the interview with **Ivan Kander** (Lucky 9 Studios) in between. I came across a short film he made called *Von Doom* that gives a take on the origins of Doctor Doom. I thought it would be good to include a completely outside perspective on *The Fantastic Four* but from someone who obviously understands the source material and works within the film industry. Before contacting Ito, my plan was to end with

Kander. I thought that ending with a younger and fresher view would be a good and unexpected way to close the collection. That would also prevent Corman from having the final word. Letting Corman speak last might seem unfair to some of the other interviewees. Placing Kander's interview between Eichinger and Stan Lee helped break up the rough quality of both interviews. Also, I thought it would be more appropriate to let **Stan Lee** (co-creator of the Fantastic Four) have the last word. I briefly considered including the Eichinger and Stan Lee material as an appendix, but not only did that seem disrespectful in some way, it also felt inappropriate since both men are so central to the story of *The Fantastic Four*, albeit in different ways.

Although I would have loved to talk to Stan Lee, he was in ill health and passed as I was making my way to the last interviews. Nevius knew him and said he would see about arranging an interview for me. As I recounted much earlier, he cautioned me, however, that Stan Lee would probably not want to talk about *The Fantastic Four*, so I planned to ask him questions about the Fantastic Four more as a comic. Ironically, I probably got a better and more relevant interview with Stan Lee via Ito because Stan Lee was in better health in those days when Ito first interviewed him, and Ito got him to talk much more about that early movie than the big-budget one from 2005 that Stan Lee thought was the actual focus of the interview.

Ways to Connect, Set Up, and Move from One Interview to Another

While the interviews in *Forsaken* can be read separately, I wanted the collection to feel like an integrated whole and for the interviews to flow into and out of one another like the segments of a river or waves in a larger ocean. Sometimes that linkage came naturally at the end and/or beginning of an interview, and other times I created the bridge by moving content around within an interview. While not all of the interviews link up as well as the examples I am going to share, opportunities for linkages are still good to keep in mind, look for, and try to create in the editing phase.

Here is the end of the Mick Strawn interview that precedes the interview with Pete Von Sholly.

*

You gotta talk to Peter Von Sholly. He is the most interesting being to talk to. Peter is an old friend of mine and I sucked him into this horrible situation. He rides that line between storyboards and working in the comic book world. He brings those two things together.

I'm looking at him on IMDb and, wow, he's got a million credits. Gee whiz.

He is the best storyboard artist that's ever existed.

*

At the end of the Kat Green interview that precedes the interview with Alex Hyde-White this question arose.

*

Will you do this as an audiobook, too?

I haven't thought it out that far. You never know.

I think that would be great. You can get Alex to read it.

*

At the end of the Alex Hyde-White interview that precedes the interview with Joseph Culp, I made a connection to the previous interview with Green and the one to come with Culp.

*

I'll leave that as is. Anything else you want to add?

I like audiobooks. What I'm doing now is producing audiobooks through Audible and other publishers. I'm bringing all sorts of stories and turning them into audio. I feel like I'm the Roger Corman of audiobook production, which is absolutely lovely because there's no camera and there's a lot less drama. We produce about fifty to sixty audiobooks a year. We've been doing it for about six years now. If you're an independent author or you know independent authors, you would want to know a company like us because we would bring voice to your work and that's very satisfying.

Kat Green and I were talking about Punch Audio doing _The Fantastic Four_. That's one way to get the movie released in some version. I know Joseph Culp would like to redo his lines, and I have a copy of the screenplay . . .

*

At the end of the Mark Sikes interview that precedes the Roger Corman interview, Sikes talks about interviewing Corman.

*

Roger at first declined to be interviewed as well. I know he's had some bad experiences with documentaries. I was able to take another route to getting him to talk. Did you interview him?

No, but I'm working on it.

I don't think he wants to talk about it. Evidently, he feels the documentary was unkind to him, so the film is probably a sore subject.

*

Although you can always produce your own end comment to create a path to the next interview, that technique is a little heavy handed and would become repetitive through the course of an entire book. I think it's better to use the interviewee's words.

Working with Editors

Unless you are the sole author of a work and have your own publishing company or webpage, you will not control and have final say, end-to-end and start to finish, over the finished version that the public will read. With rare exceptions, there will be an intermediate point or points somewhere along the way and your work will pass beneath the eyes and through the hands or inboxes of others. Good editors will help you bring out the best version of your work. They may make or suggest macro-level changes such as eliminating/reordering entire paragraphs or paragraph sequences. Or they may see possibilities for micro-level choices like word substitutions or small punctuation tweaks. If nothing else, another set of eyes will help catch and fix tiny proofreading errors that might slip by you. However, editing is not always about finding and fixing mistakes—that is more of what I think of as proofreading—but about enhancing the piece and taking it to the next level: unacceptable to acceptable, good to great, great to excellent, or even excellent to timeless.

Keep in mind that many/most editors are in the same situation as many/most writers: overworked and underpaid or not paid at all. I try to keep the same standard as when I visit a fast food restaurant. I expect minimum service from people making the minimum, but I do expect some sort of service. Thus, with editors I have minimal expectations, but I do expect minimum response and courtesy. If someone belittles me or consistently does not respond, I exit. Editors who seem to be in a constant state of turmoil, distress, disorganization, disruption, conflict, and are always lagging behind, overwhelmed and overloaded, should be avoided unless you either like drama, their work style meshes well with yours, or you are getting a tremendous professional and/or financial boost from working with them. When I say "tremendous," I mean next-level and lifechanging, not just more of what you have already accomplished. Differentiate between reasons and excuses. Accept the former and reject the latter. Stuff happens and people have life events, so give grace and be understanding. However, if there is always something going on, some problem, and it becomes a consistent professional interference, I suggest exiting the situation.

Increasingly, the kind of relationship I have with individual publishing venues matters more and more to me. When you find a good editor and develop a good relationship with a press or publication, stay with them. When you have a bad experience and it seems such experiences will be the pattern—once is an event and twice is a pattern—and not the exception, cut your ties and move forward to a new situation as soon as you can. The money or prestige may be the same or even less, but if the relationship is better, then the change is better. If working with a particular publishing venture doesn't make me feel good or at least okay, I don't do it. To date, I have not found a powerful enough incentive to make me stay in a bad situation with an editor or publication any longer than I absolutely have to.

The most egregious editorial error of my own work that I have thus far encountered was the interviewee's name misspelled in each and every appearance in a publication. Even though I sent the interview and all supporting materials with the interviewee's name correctly spelled, the editor, or someone acting with their authority, went into the final draft that I submitted and changed each and every instance of the interviewee's name from a correct to an incorrect spelling. How did that happen? The final responsibility rests with the last and highest person in the chain.

A bad editor is worse than no editor because they can be counterproductive and generally slow down and problematize what can already be a slow and challenging enough process.

Although I have divided editing into the micro and macro levels, from a practical standpoint, I separate editing into these three main types of editing suggestions. Category one: changes that I definitely agree with and, therefore, always make whether it's a quick micro-level proofreading error or a larger macro-level idea that will take some time such as adding in an explanatory paragraph or two to a piece (that's usually more for an essay than an interview, but the principle stands true). Category two: changes that I don't see a need to make, but don't mind making. Such changes neither add to nor detract from the piece, I don't have a strong feeling about these changes, and they are not time consuming to make, so I just say "yes" and move ahead. Category three: changes I do not want to make. Occasionally, they may be objectively incorrect. More often, they lower the quality, in my opinion, of the writing. In response to these changes, I provide a rationale for why I chose the original word, made an unconventional choice, phrased the passages the way

I did, or want to keep the sentence the editor suggests I delete, and so on. I may also explain why I think the proposed change is inferior to what I originally wrote. I am not confrontational; I just explain my thinking. Sometimes the editor sees what I am saying or understands a point they did not understand before and agrees with me. Sometimes the editor responds back with a counterpoint or perspective that *I* had not considered and I reverse my thinking and say, "I hadn't thought of that. Good point. I'll make that change." Or sometimes I may have a counter-proposal and say, "I see what you are saying and I'll make a change, but I think a different change other than the one you propose may be more effective in accomplishing that" and then I'll state my new idea for that change. Conversations with editors can be something of a negotiation but it should feel like each party is working for the same outcome: the best version of the interview. It should feel like neither a struggle nor a battle.

It's fairly common to get to look at a draft of the final piece and/or respond to comments and suggested changes before it is published, whether in print or online, but that is not always the case. I have found just as—or even more—often, editors will not take that kind of time and will make whatever changes they see fit. You will only find out after the fact when you read your published piece. If you are not entirely happy with what you see, you don't have much recourse. If it's a print publication, then that's the end of the road. If it's an online piece, you can email them and see if you can get them to reverse their change(s) or restore what you originally wrote and see if they even respond. My advice is to skip composing and sending that email, take it in stride, and move on with your writing life. That emotion and energy you expend for a possibly futile course of action will be better spent writing, researching, and setting up the next interview. The only exception is that if it's an online piece and you see an obvious and clear error (yours or theirs). In that case, you should probably contact the publication and let them know; they may even be grateful. However, if you hear nothing back, I recommend what I said several sentences ago: Let it go and move on, no matter how awful the experience, or, perhaps, especially if it's been an awful experience. Like anything and everything else that didn't go how we wanted or expected, we have to learn to live with it. In most instances, it matters less the more time moves on.

Remember, sometimes the juice is not worth the squeeze.

Backtracking

As I was conducting interviews for *Forsaken*, I picked up information that I wanted to confirm or a comment I wanted to get someone's take on. For example, a question came up about whether The Thing's costume had a cool suit or not, so I backtracked and emailed people I had already spoken with who might know and included that information in their interviews. Robert Alan Beuth knew Ian Trigger who played a key acting role in *The Fantastic Four* but had since passed. Beuth shared some good memories and I thought it would be nice to backtrack and contact some other people who had known him, get their thoughts, and place those recollections in their interviews as a sort of tribute and remembrance. Where there were matters of dispute, such as the cool suit (Everett Burrell swore there was, but everyone else I spoke to swore there was not), I tried not to get too much into "he said / she said," keep running back and forth between or among interviewees, and stir up trouble. Or, when Stan Lee passed, I started bringing that up in interviews but I did not backtrack and ask everyone I already talked to what they thought about his passing and/or legacy. It's okay to go back. It can even be good to go back, but don't go back too much or you'll never be able to move forward.

You have to draw things to a close at some point.

www.ingramcontent.com/pod-product-compliance
Ingram Content Group UK Ltd.
Pitfield, Milton Keynes, MK11 3LW, UK
UKHW021907190726
13853UKWH00002B/551